Blood Sisters

A Tale of Adoption, Thalassemia,
Sisterhood and Miracles

Jamie M Dailey
7/21/2015

For Serenity, Betty June and Belle
Sisters through and through

CONTENTS

This book would not have been possible without the support and encouragement of my husband, Matthew Dailey.

Thank you to my sons, Matthew, Dean and Donovan Dailey for accepting our decision to add to our family through adoption and loving your sisters without limits or hesitation.

Thank you to my daughter in love, Nicole for being willing to embrace this crazy family as your own and adding the first member of the next generation, Jackson.

Thank you to both sets of grandparent for support and babysitting.

Thank you to Chinese Children's Adoption International for smoothly facilitating our first two adoptions.

Thank you to Children's Hospital of Pittsburgh and Children's Hospital of Philadelphia for expert medical care and guidance as we navigate the girls' medical needs.

Thank you to the members of Adoptive Parents of Children with Thalassemia for teaching me so much and being a sounding board.

Thank you to the Cooley's Anemia Foundation for fighting for a cure.

And finally, thank you to my sister for teaching me how strong of a bond sisters can have. I'm glad we didn't trade you for a goat.

'His shoe is untied.' That was the thought going thru my head as I sat on the front pew of the church during my son's wedding. 'His shoe is untied and it's not my problem anymore, its Nikki's.'

Not my problem. He was a grown man and I was out of a job. Sure he would still need me sometimes, but not like when he was little. He and his two brothers were men. Dean was getting married and it was the beginning of the end of a parenting era.

Were we ready for it?

The short answer is 'No'. The long answer is the story that follows.

Chapter 1

It takes courage to grow up and become who you really are.
e. e. cummings

As a high school junior I was assigned the task to write an essay on what direction I wanted to go in my life. It was the standard 'What I want to be when I grow up' assignment. The paper was returned to me as unrealistic and I had to rewrite it. Why? It was because my life's goal was to be a wife and mother. I wanted several children and I wanted raising those children to be my full time job. Unfortunately in the eyes of my English teacher that was unrealistic and naive. Mr. Cleveland, you were wrong.

Matt and I married when we were pretty young. He was 20 and had just finished his sophomore year of college with two more to go. I was 19. We were young and had our whole lives ahead of us. We thought we wanted a houseful of children, 6 seemed to be our ideal number.

Matt finished college and headed to grad school. I was working for a dentist as a chairside assistant. Our first son, Mattie, was born the day before I turned 23 and I became a stay at home mom.

Less than 2 years after Mattie was born along came Dean AND Donovan. Identical twin boys born when Mattie was 22 months old, gave us 3 boys in less than two years. Life was hectic to say the least. My mother-in-law took a year off work to help out. Lots of days it took both of us to keep them fed and clean.

I'm not going to lie, as they got older, we had fun. I loved being the mom of boys. There was always an adventure just around the corner. We went camping and caught tadpoles. There were plenty of sports and activities going on. They earned the nickname, 'The Boybarians'. The idea of six kids seemed less than ideal while they were little. It was hectic but we still managed to have a good time.

Since dad is an accountant and we homeschooled we decided to take a trip around Pennsylvania while dad worked the long hours of tax season. The boys and I took off in our full size van with a budget of $100 a day. We drove thru Allegheny National Forest, saw some elk, saw the Pennsylvania Grand Canyon, visited an apiary, and lots of other out of the way places in our home state.

While I was busy being mom to the growing boys, dad was busy growing his career. During these years he was working really hard for his family. After completing his MBA, he earned his CPA and became a partner at his office. He coached Little League and was treasurer of the League for a few years.

We were a young family and family was the most important thing. Our house had a revolving door during those years for various friends and family members. The boys had friends that spent a lot of time at our house, especially Timmy that remains a close friend to this day.

My nephew spent some summers with us and we hosted a young boy from Belarus a few summers thru an organization called Children of Chernobyl. Sometimes they were all there at the same time. Those summers we instituted a matching shirt policy, that is we chose a special matching shirts for all of us to wear during big outings. 5 boys, dad and mom headed out all in matching yellow shirts for an amusement park, zoo, museum or ball game. On one such outing we must have been quite a site, 5 boys 10,9,8,7 & 7 in bright yellow shirts trailing behind us in our bright yellow shirts. A dear, sweet elderly nun came up to me, took my hand and with tears glistening in her eyes said, "Bless you my child."

I knew we were blessed but I had no idea the blessings that still lie ahead for me at that time. I often think of that nun.

Fast forward to the boys getting a little older and life hit a predictable rhythm. We thought maybe we could handle one more. We tried the biological route. I had my tubal reversed. Things just never seemed to work out. We were chasing technology in an attempt to have another child. We came to the realization that the child, not the pregnancy, was our goal so we started researching adoption. It turned out God's plan for our family was to add a daughter born in China.

The first people we told about our plan to adopt were our sons. By now they were 13, 11 and 11 and given to having strong opinions about everything. Dean said, "We can name her Serenity." The name was perfect and it stuck. They say they knew what we were planning and they were not surprised by our announcement. I'm not so sure about that.

Dean, the groom from earlier, was so committed to the process; he walked each step with me. If I was mailing something, he went into the post office with me. If I was dropping off forms at the social workers, he was at my side. He even traveled to China with us to bring her home. He wanted to hold her first, but he had to settle for third! On his wedding day, she was the flower girl and at the reception he had a special dance with her to the song "You'll Be in My Heart" from Tarzan.

Serenity was 11 months old when she came to our family. Matt was 38, I was 37, Mattie was 14, Dean and Donovan were 12, and we thought our family was complete, 3 Boybarians and our Girlzilla. Maybe our plan was to be a family of 6 instead of having 6 kids.

Life goes on as life does. There were, first days of school, first dates, and first jobs, drivers licenses, proms, birthday parties and graduations and then, Dean got married.

We were happy, thrilled even. His wife, Nikki, is a terrific woman and we feel so blessed to have her in our family. But where did the time go? When did we stop being a young family? We weren't ready to start the empty nest.

Mattie was 21, Dean and Donovan were 18 and Serenity was 7 at the wedding and turned 8 a few weeks later.

At first we thought it was no big deal. It was just the natural progression of life. You raise your children to leave you. That's the deal. Parenting done properly works you out of a job.

But we liked that job. I mean really liked that job. And just like 'you never want a drink of water until the well runs dry', it wasn't until we saw the inevitable end that we realized how much being parents and having little kids around meant to us.

So what's a mom to do when facing unemployment? It's simple, really. Have more kids. So that is what we did. After a few years of back and forth, should we/shouldn't we, we did. A call to the same adoption agency we used to adopt Serenity, fill out a few forms and we were back in the game.

Chapter 2

Become a student of change. It is the
only thing that will remain constant.
Anthony J. D'Angelo

In the time since we adopted Serenity the Chinese
adoption world had changed. When we adopted Serenity
most children coming to the US from China were healthy
baby girls. China began to recognize their growing
gender imbalance and put the brakes on healthy young
girls being adopted internationally. What had been a
steady stream in 2004 became a trickle in 2011. For
Serenity we waited 9 months from the time our paperwork
went to China until we received her information.
Basically, China took a look at us, chose a daughter for us,
and sent us her information. Like so many other daughters
from China adopted into US families, she is the perfect
daughter for our family. We received Serenity's 'referral'
and 6 weeks later we were on a plane to China to get her.

For this second adoption the wait for a healthy
young girl was at least 7 years with the wait getting longer
and longer with no end in sight. At 45 and 44, we didn't
think that was the right way to go, but we were committed
to adopting another Chinese daughter. We really thought
having our daughters share a heritage was important so we
started looking over the list of special needs to consider.

There were so many health issues to consider and
they ran the gamut from minor to severe. Some were
cosmetic and some were life-threatening. We weren't sure
where to start. I did some internet searches but I knew that
real life experience was what I needed to hear about.

When we went to China to bring Serenity home
we didn't go alone. We traveled with 5 other families, of

those 5 we still keep in touch with 3 families and 2 of them had adopted again thru the special needs program. So I reached out to them for guidance, they didn't disappoint.

One of the most common special needs coming out of China seemed to be cleft lip and palate. Our friends Kelly and Jason had brought home two sons with this need. Those guys are great! Their energy and enthusiasm are boundless and when I am with them they remind me of Dean and Donovan as little boys. Kelly and I had a great email exchange that confirmed to me that cleft wasn't a need we wanted to consider.

Another couple Michelle and Don adopted the oldest girl in our group. She is older than our Serenity by just a few weeks. Once home with her they discovered that she had beta thalassemia minor, a condition none of us had ever heard of. After learning about thalassemia they felt comfortable enough to adopt a son with a different form of thalassemia. After talking and texting with Michelle we didn't think thalassemia was a condition we wanted to put on our list either, mainly because it seemed so involved and time consuming. I think God probably laughed out loud at that moment. So we filled out our medical conditions checklist and set out to prepare our dossier, that is all the necessary paperwork for China.

The special needs program is divided into two categories, Log In Date only and Special Focus. The more minor needs are reserved for families that already have their dossier logged in at the China Center for Children's Welfare and Adoption which is China's central agency dealing with adoption. Cleft lip and palate fall into that category as well as minor heart issues and other less involved needs. The special focus program is where you will find the more severe needs. Needs that will require ongoing care or multiple needs will fall into this category. You can be matched with a child from the special focus

We had lots of needs we were open to so we set out to finish our dossier because we thought we would be matched with a log-in only file. Our particular agency matched files with waiting families as they received the files from China. Since they have a partnership with orphanages in Henan province they get files several times a month. They use the date you file your medical needs checklist to set your place in line. At the time the wait for a little girl with a minor need was 12-18 months. The files that don't fall into anyone's waiting checklist go on their website. The closer we got to completing our dossier and having it ready to send to China, the more I stalked the website.

We had started our dossier in the summer of 2012, by February 2013 it was all done and at the agency awaiting final review before its trip to Beijing.

Matt is a CPA in an accounting firm that does over 3000 tax returns. During the period of mid January to May I work in his office. Many days I would work the same hours he did, 9-7. One of the best things about that is we have lunch and dinner together. It was on just such a day that I saw Belle's picture for the first time.

I checked the agency's website on my Smartphone while Matt ordered us a pizza for dinner. There were no new additions to the waiting child list. There had been a few little boys that had piqued my interest. They had all been log-in only so we weren't able to pursue them, plus Matt had his heart set on another little girl. I checked the website at least once a day and usually two or three times.

After enjoying a really good pizza, we headed back to the office for our evening hours. Once back in my little office I thought I would check one more time. You know, just in case.

BOOM! There were new little faces there and there were two young girls, Qing and Qang. I printed the two pages out and ran down the steps to show Matt. He told me to call our agency. Back up the stairs to my office I hurriedly called our agency. Since they are in Colorado and we are in Pennsylvania they were still in the office. When I inquired about the girls I was told they were both still available but I had to choose because we could only have one file at a time. Qing had the same birthday as my sister so I chose her.

Isn't that silly? Something as random as an assigned birthday made me choose one over the other. But God is in the little, random things as much as He is in the big earth shattering things. He is in the flutter of a butterfly's wings just as He is in the strong winds of a hurricane. Qing's special needs were listed as Post-Op Megaureter, Patent Foramen Ovule and Anemia. Qang's needs were joint related. But Qing shared a birthday with my little sister so I turned left instead of right and that made all the difference.

Chapter 3
No Job is finished until the Paperwork is Done

There are a few significant steps in adoption from China, but they can go in different order.

The first is finally getting your dossier (stack of paperwork) together and sending it to China. That is called DTC, dossier to China.

After it gets to Beijing it is logged into the system that is called LID, log in date.

The second is being matched with a child, called referral.

Then there is sending in your Letter of Intent, LOI and receiving Pre-Approval, PA.

In our case we completed our dossier and then found our daughter. Then we were LOI, PA, DTC and LID in that order.

Now for a huge step, LOA! The LOA is the letter of acceptance or letter seeking confirmation. It is an official letter from China asking if we accept Qing's referral to be our daughter.

We signed it and sent it back to the agency PDQ. (pretty darn quick) aka the same day we received it we overnighted it back.

But I am getting ahead of myself so let's go back a few steps.

The agency emailed Qing's file to us. The file contained information about her health and development. I spent the rest of the evening pouring over every detail in the file. I did some quick research on the two main conditions listed, megaureter and PFO.

She had surgery several months before to correct the megaureter. The PFO, patent foramen ovule, amounted to a tiny opening between the two atriums in the heart. For most people that opening closes at birth but plenty of people are walking around with the opening still there. Qing still had the opening.

The last diagnosis in her file was anemia. Her hemoglobin was listed at 4.6. Normal hemoglobin would be between 11 and 14, so she was very anemic, but that seemed the least of her special needs.

We had our family doctor look at her file. My mother in law, who is a nurse practitioner, also looked at her file. They both noted how low her hemoglobin was but thought there could be many, varying from diet related to the surgery for the megaureter.

We had 72 hours to review her file and make a decision. When we called the agency back to say we wanted to pursue adopting Qing they told me there was a long list interested in her if we had said no.

Fortunately our dossier was already at our agency so preparing the Letter of Intent was pretty simple. We had to do a care plan and just a few more things. We completed it as soon as we could and sent the LOI mid April.

While waiting for pre-approval from China I continued to research the two main issues in Qing's file. I even ordered a pulse oximeter to monitor her oxygen levels during the plane ride home. I thought I was getting prepared to bring home a 'heart baby'. I was wrong.

The agency we were using has a partnership with Henan Province. That means they, as an organization, gives special support to the orphanages there in exchange for the opportunity to place their children. It works out very well for both parties involved and most agencies doing Chinese adoption have similar arrangements. Since our Qing was in a special orphan care center we were able to take over sponsorship of her. We sent a small donation each month in exchange for updates. It was in one of those updates we first saw 'blood transfusion'.

At this point I jumped in with both feet. I sent her file to my friend Michelle; she has two children with thalassemia. She looked over the file and thought it looked like it could be thalassemia. My next step was to contact Children's Hospital of Philadelphia Thalassemia Center, and Cooley's Anemia Foundation.

There are seven CDC Thalassemia centers in the United States. They are in Philadelphia, Boston, Chicago, Atlanta, Houston, Los Angeles and Oakland. We are fortunate to be within a day's drive of Philadelphia. So consulting with them was a good step for us to get confirmation of what we suspected.

Qing had thalassemia.

We weren't sure what type of thalassemia she had with the limited information given to us. But Philadelphia gave us pretty good information and a preliminary diagnosis.

Qing had thalassemia.

One of the special needs we decided we didn't want to mark.

Qing had thalassemia.

We had decided thalassemia was potentially too time consuming and too scary to consider.

Qing had thalassemia.

But in the few weeks since we received pre-approval from China to adopt, she had stopped being Qing to us. She had become Belle, our daughter. Qing was an orphan in China with a potentially life threatening blood disorder. Belle was my baby who needed me and needed me fast.

Chapter 4
Lead, follow, or get out of the way.
Laurence J. Peter

From the CDC website:
Thalassemia is an inherited (i.e., passed from parents to children through genes) blood disorder caused when the body doesn't make enough of a protein called hemoglobin, an important part of red blood cells. When there isn't enough hemoglobin, the body's red blood cells don't function properly and they last shorter periods of time, so there are fewer healthy red blood cells traveling in the bloodstream.
Red blood cells carry oxygen to all the cells of the body. Oxygen is a sort of food that cells use to function. When there are not enough healthy red blood cells, there is also not enough oxygen delivered to all the other cells of the body, which may cause a person to feel tired, weak or short of breath. This is a condition called anemia. People with thalassemia may have mild or severe anemia. Severe anemia can damage organs and lead to death.

You know how you never want to get between a mother bear and her cubs? This applies here too.

I do believe the orphanages in China do all they can for their kids but the fact remains that they have limited resources. There is a chronic blood shortage for a variety of reasons and sometimes the government forces the soldiers to donate. As a result the kids don't get transfused to the standards we have in America. We weren't sure how often or how much our daughter was getting transfused.

We began our efforts to expedite the process to get her home. If the road to hell is paved with good intentions, the road to China is paved with lots and lots of red tape. Every clearance and approval costs money and time from the US clear through the Chinese government. We got used to writing large checks but, the good news was our dossier was ready to go to China.

Cooley's Anemia Foundation is an organization in the United States dedicated to thalassemia. I contacted the Patient's Services Manager, Eileen Scott, and she sent us a letter explaining the urgency of getting our daughter home to receive proper treatment.

Children's Hospital of Philadelphia provided a similar letter from the head of the Thalassemia Center. I sent copies of those letters to our agency to send them with our dossier. Our dossier was sent to China and logged in April 24th. (LID)

The next step was to receive the Letter of Acceptance (LOA). At the time the wait was around 45 days. Our agency was not hopeful we would receive it any sooner.

Since the time of Serenity's adoption the United States had signed the Hague Convention on International Adoption. It is an agreement between countries intended to stop child trafficking. As a result it slows down the timeline for international adoption. We had Serenity's picture for six weeks until we were able to meet her. When we received her referral we were told it would take 4-6 weeks to travel. Now the expected wait was 6 months, way too long for a medically fragile child.

In the mean time I was researching like crazy. I was fortunate enough to find a terrific Facebook group especially for parents with adopted children with thalassemia. I have long held the opinion if you want the nitty-gritty on any disease find a mom whose child has that been a member of that group now for about 2 years (depending on when you are reading this). The best way to describe it is they (we) are like a big, loud, pushy, nosey, wonderful, loving family. Through them I learned the best way to expedite and what to expect once we were home.

Part of any international adoption process is dealing with the branch of the United States government dealing with immigration. *Joy.* During the process you are fingerprinted and fill out several forms, and then you are assigned an officer for your case. Like any other branch of society there are helpful and not so helpful officers. This time we drew a not so helpful officer. The officer's job is to review your paperwork and either approve or deny your application to bring an orphan into the United States and declare them your 'next of kin'. (I haven't ever heard of a denial) The speed they accomplish this task at is solely their discretion. Officially adoption cases take priority, but which adoption case is up to them. She was not at all sympathetic and a strictly 'letter of the law' type. I had many less than helpful conversations with her.

Your application goes to a lockbox in Texas for two weeks along with your LOA before making its way to their desk. Some more helpful officers will allow you to send the application first then scan and email the precious LOA to them, saving you two weeks wait. This officer warned me not to do that because she would not accept the scanned LOA. The last conversation we had went something like this.

"Is the child dying?"

"She has a life threatening condition that needs proper treatment."

"But is she dying?"

"She will be if we don't get her home as soon as we can."

'Is she dying?"

"Sister, we're all dying. Life is a terminal condition and none of us get out of it alive."

I was so angry I could hear my heart pounding in my ears. One of the worst things about cell phones is the lack of the ability to slam the receiver down thus notifying the party on the other end of your displeasure. You just can't hit the 'end' button hard enough. Nonetheless, I hung up on her knowing she was a brick wall.

I had been in contact with our congressman to help us with the US side of the adoption. I found the most Pro-Life congressman we had to help us. Our contact person was a woman named Rachel. Even she said our officer was impossible to work with. I'm not sure what magic happened behind the scenes but we were reassigned to another officer, a much more sympathetic, human officer.

Somewhere in the magical glow of getting a new USCIS officer we received our LOA. What should have taken 45-60 days took 25 days. Our agency was pretty surprised we got it three weeks sooner than expected. But unfortunately the time we wasted arguing with Officer 'Is she dying' costs us the two weeks we could have sent in the application early.

After dealing with our first officer and getting nowhere I was feeling like we were hitting walls in expediting. I felt pretty ineffective in my human efforts. And like I have done so many other times in this process I just kept praying. But my prayers changed. I fell asleep each night crying out to God. He had to do the expediting, not me, not my agency, not China. He parted the Red Sea; He could cut the red tape. And He did. I was checking my email Monday May 20, 2013 not expecting much, we were only on day 25. And there it was, right there in front of me; a miracle. I was caught off guard, 25 days from LID to LOA that is smoking fast. Expedite, boom!

To quote my Mamow Aggie, "Thank You, Jesus"

We were told to expect travel in 10-14 weeks. That would have put us leaving for China in mid to late August.

The US Consulate that handles adoptions in China is in Guangzhou (gwan-jo). I had been in email contact with them regarding expediting our case. They were willing to accept our letters from Cooley's and Children's Hospital Philadelphia. What normally takes 2 weeks took two days. And if the US Consulate in Guangzhou expedites then Beijing usually expedites the Travel Approval.

10-14 weeks became a few days short of 6 weeks to Travel Approval. June 28th we received the call from our agency telling us TA had just arrived from China. Matt, Serenity and I had stopped for lunch at a noodle restaurant before going to Whole Foods that particular Friday. After we ordered, Serenity and I found a table and got our drinks. Matt brought our food over and we had just started eating when I noticed I had missed a call. It was a Colorado number so I knew it was our agency. I quickly redialed and got the good news. I will never know if those noodles were good because I was too excited to eat. The agency was once again pretty surprised how fast it happened, but we had been working hard behind the scenes to get things happening.

Now we needed a consulate appointment. Of course we requested the first available appointment which would have been July 31st. We were able to get August 6th. We would finally be able to meet Belle July 29, and we would leave for China July 24.

The annual reunion for Serenity's adoption group was planned for July 13-20 on Edisto Island, North Carolina. I'm sure lots of folks thought we were just a little nuts to be undertaking a week long beach vacation RIGHT BEFORE we went to China for two weeks on an adoption trip. I know they did because, truthfully, so did I.

But I have never been accused of being level headed and having a firm grip on reasonable and rational thinking. I mean, honestly? I was a 46 year old woman adopting a 19 month old baby! At a time plenty of friends were welcoming grandchildren, I was actively pursuing a tiny tot halfway around the world. How rational and reasonable could I have been? But then again, I never want to be so level-headed and rational I miss out on the wonder all around me. I want to run headlong into life embracing the mystery and beauty of all it can be.

Chapter 5

You'll need coffee shops and sunsets
and road trips. Airplanes and passports
and new songs and old songs, but
people more than anything else. You
will need other people and you will
need to be that other person to someone
else, a living breathing screaming
invitation to believe better things." —
Jamie Tworkowski

So why a week at a beach in South Carolina for
her reunion right before a two week adoption trip to
China? Actually this is a very important trip, for many
reasons. But the 4 biggest reasons are (in order of age):
1. Grace
2. Serenity
3. Katie
4. Madeline

They are four little girls that shared their first
months together. Our Serenity has no known biological
connections. These girls share a history, a story. Serenity
calls them her "China Sisters". I love that phrase. This
trip is a chance for them to all reconnect and nurture the
bond they share. That summer on the cusp of double digit

age, it involved lots of giggling and squealing. But it is all good.

And the parents? Well, let me tell you, Oh my, the glorious support! It is so special to share something as precious and intimate as those first moments with your child. Our families started as strangers in an airport but during the two week adoption trip we melded into family.

When we first started thinking about adopting again, these were some of the first people we talked to. When we were considering which special needs we were comfortable with. Boom, text Kelly. Noreen was quick to offer to help us with adoption travel since she worked for a major airline. Think Belle may have Thalassemia; Michelle is in the know since she is 1. A pediatric nurse and 2. Has two kids with different forms of thalassemia. I mean how awesome to have that kind of support?

And the dads, well the dads do what dads do. They joke and guffaw and love being crazy uncles to the kids. Jason makes sweet tea; Don cooks low country boil, and Jim and Matt love to talk sports. And Jim helped us arrange our trips to and from China.

Every year we laugh about the same stories. The nervousness at meeting the girls, the hallway parties, Dean eating squid, McDonalds that delivered to our hotel, Chinese hot dogs, the trip to the zoo. It is a reunion in every sense of the word. And now, to add to the fun? There are now 3 'too cute for color TV' Chinese little brothers thrown into the mix.

The first thing I said when I found out that our consulate appt was Aug 6 instead of July 31 was, 'Well, God must think Serenity's reunion is pretty important too.' Hey! Who am I to argue?

It was amazing to watch the girls reconnect. I'm not sure 'reconnect' the right word because they walked into the rooms and acted like one of them had just gone to the kitchen and came back. It seemed like a natural connection that had never been broken by mere distance.

During that trip we went to the beach, took the girls to paint ceramics, ate some awesome seafood and listened to lots and lots of giggling.

Also during that week we had our agency's travel call. Of course, the phone was on speakerphone with all the 'aunts and uncles' were right there at the dining room table with us.

When I think back to the strangers we all were when we met in those airports of San Francisco and Hong Kong and compare it to the extended family we are today, I am so humbled. I thought I was gaining a daughter when we went to China, in reality I gained so much more. I have been blessed, indeed.

Chapter 6

I don't care how much money I gotta spend, Got to get back to my baby   The Boxtops

July 17th while we were on Edisto we received our final travel arrangements. In anticipation of this trip to China Matt had been working on gathering up hotel points to help pay for our 2 weeks of hotel stays. He did a crazy good job and our total cost for the two weeks was less than $300 and that included an executive suite for four nights in our last city.

Our itinerary looked like this:

7/23 Off to Pittsburgh for the night before our 5:45am flight

7/24 Leave U.S. for Beijing.

7/25 Arrive in Beijing

7/26 Tour Beijing.   This will be our 27th Wedding Anniversary. What a way to celebrate!

Tiananmen Square, Forbidden City, Hutong Tour, and Acrobatics show.

7/27 Tour Beijing.

Great Wall.

7/28 Depart Beijing for Zhengzhou

7/29 Today we will meet our daughter.

7/30 Today Dang Yu Qing will be officially adopted into our family

7/31 Free day.

8/1 Official paperwork in the morning, Visit Kaifeng Social Welfare Institute.

8/2 Free day, receive Belle's passport.
8/3 Leave Zhengzhou for Guangzhou
8/4 Paperwork Party
8/5 Medical day. Physical for Belle
8/6 Consulate appointment
8/7 Receive Belle's visa packet. Depart Guangzhou for Hong Kong for an overnight
8/8 Depart Hong Kong for the USA.
WELCOME HOME BELLE!

The trip to China was pretty emotional for Serenity and I. At 10 years old this was her first trip back to China. Before her trip she had expressed fear she would have to meet her birth family. She seemed relieved when I told her there was no way for us to find them. When she is older I am sure she will change her mind but for now that was her biggest fear.

After spending the night at the Pittsburgh Airport Hyatt, we happily boarded our plane for a 12 hour flight to Beijing. We were glad we sprung for Economy Plus for such a long trip. The flight itself was pretty uneventful. We dozed on and off. Watched a few movies, most notably The Croods, ate a few times and it was touchdown in China.

Coming back to China is always a very profound experience for me. I am so proud of my America and all it stands for, but China is such an old civilization. And political differences aside, it is a beautiful land. Oh sure, you can pick apart anything, but look deeper and see what is really there. See the people, listen to the cadence of everyday life, and watch mom and grandma walking with the son or daughter and it is a beautiful picture. It could be happening anywhere, even in our hometown. But it isn't happening in my homeland, it is Serenity's homeland and that makes it all the more special.

I was watching Serenity closely. I looked for clues of how this experience was affecting her. Little Miss handled it the way she handles everything, with joy and exuberance. She loves China, everything about China...

Well, almost everything...on our first day of touring Beijing we faced the Westernized woman's greatest adversary.....The Squatty Potty! My little Princess would have none of that! When confronted, she declared she would hold it! And she said so in a manner that left no wavering in her decision. I, being made of weaker fiber, availed myself of the opportunity to 'experience China'.

We had a busy day, breakfast at the hotel buffet with its wide assortment of offerings, both Western and Chinese, and then a bus ride to 'Old' Beijing. We boarded rickshaws and toured the hutongs. The hutongs are old style neighborhoods.....just Google it, it's hard to describe. We went to visit Mrs. Wu, a 70 something resident of the hutongs. She told us something about her life in the hutongs. It was humbling and lovely as she served us tea and snacks while she talked about her semi-arranged marriage and raising her 3 children there. She told us that 6 families share the same courtyard AND communal bathroom. Before that I was buying the romanticism of 'Old Beijing' and the community spirit it offered. I was even willing to arrange marriages for my kids, but she lost me at community bathroom. At the end Serenity spoke to her in the little Mandarin she knows. And when we left Little Miss declared she WILL learn Mandarin! Mrs. Wu said that is the one thing she would like the children that leave China to take with them, their native language.

From the hutongs back on our tour bus to the silk factory, and like every factory tour you have ever been on it was very interesting. After the tour we did some shopping and looking around. We didn't buy anything there. Oh don't worry; we did stimulate the local economy plenty when the time was right. Once back on the bus

George, our guide, took us to a Chinese restaurant for lunch. It was there Serenity encountered the aforementioned bathroom. Serenity was severely grossed out and George said he would take us to a better one. We needed to work on George's definition of better.

Tiananmen Square and the Forbidden City were awe-inspiring beyond what pictures can convey. We were walking on stones laid decades before Columbus sailed the ocean blue. We were there during the height of summer and summer tourism. The crowds in the Forbidden City were incredible. Even on the great expanse of Tiananmen Square the sheer number of people was daunting for us.

After touring it was back to the hotel for a cooling respite and a swim. Serenity made friends with the other little girl in our group that was also born in China and a similar age. They swam and played while I chatted with her mom and another mom. I think that is my favorite part of an adoption trip (besides getting the child), connecting with like minded folks on the same journey.

Once finished in the pool we went to the concierge lounge, but it wasn't anything we were interested in so we went down stairs to the main lobby and just sat around and chatted some more with our travel companions. Then back to the room for something light to eat. I was asleep by 9 which may explain why I was up at 2:30 and was not able to go back to sleep. Jet lag always kicks my butt!

The next morning we visited a jade factory. It is a tradition to pass on a piece of jade to a daughter at a significant life event like graduation, marriage or birth of a child. I had a beautiful jade bracelet to give Serenity someday so I needed one for Belle. After the jade factory it was time to go to the #1 tourist attraction in China.

The Great Wall of China was, in a word, great. It was my second time to visit because I had traveled to China with a friend on her adoption trip. For Serenity's adoption our gateway city was Hong Kong so we missed visiting the Great Wall. I was really happy to be able to go back with Matt and Serenity. Matt climbed as far as he dared in the time we had. Serenity and I climbed to the first tower then headed back down. Sitting at the Great Wall we had another heart to heart about her birth family. Dad came back down covered with sweat from his climb. We bought the best Coca-Cola we had ever tasted before getting back on the bus.

We left Beijing and her 20 million citizens to fly to the small city of Zhengzhou, population of only 9 million.

As a child of the 80's, my generation was the first to have 'at home' video games. We started with "Pong" and graduated up to Asteroids, Pacman, Ms Pacman and Donkey Kong. What does that have to do with China? Remember Frogger? Well crossing the street in Zhengzhou was a lot like that. You could not imagine the traffic. There were four lanes of traffic in each direction, but the lanes are 'more of a guideline, really'. More often than not there are 5 or 6 vehicles across in those 4 lanes, merging, honking, speeding up, and slowing down. But the traffic, while nerve-racking for this small town girl, was just a drop in the bucket compared to the sidewalks. The side'walks' are really motorways for the scooters. I guess since the road is so busy it's not safe for the scooters to drive there so they use the sidewalks.

Venturing out was something of an adventure to say the least. A few days after getting Belle we walked to a local park. And while the park was beautiful, very entertaining and relatively close, the trip there was not for the faint of heart. I was carrying Belle in the hip carrier and we were walking single file down the sidewalk. Poor Serenity had to deal with me constantly fussing about her walking, 'right in front of me!' By the time we got to the park I was a wreck. Poor kid.

The scooters came in handy another time. Matt and BJ, another dad in our group, had gone to pick up McDonald's for our two families. They had taken a taxi to McDonald's. After they had gone inside and got the food they tried to hail another cab to take them back to our hotel. They could not manage to flag down another taxi. There were several scooter riders noticed hanging about so Matt called one over and explained what he needed. Matt told him his dilemma and scooterman offered to give him a ride back to our hotel. Matt told him his friend also needed transportation so scooterman waved over a friend. Matt and BJ had the trip of their life on the back of those scooters. They gave their scooter saviors a few dollars and counted their lucky stars to be back at the hotel safe and sound.

Like I have said before China adoption had changed. Serenity's group was all from one orphanage. This adoption group of 8 families represented children from 5 different orphanages. With Serenity we got to the Civil Affairs office, the girls arrived, we were all united and we left to go back to the hotel. This time our group arrived at the Civil Affairs office and the kids trickled in one group at a time. There were three children from Belle's orphanage of Kaifeng accompanied by 2 nannies.

Seeing her was like falling in love, so wonderful there aren't words to describe it. I had fought for her, prayed for her, longed for her and now there she was. She was tiny, less than 20 lbs, and she was scared to death. I had been waiting for her but she had no idea who I was, and quite frankly, she had no interest in finding out. Dad was quick thinking and handed her a rice cracker. She decided maybe she would stick around and see what else we had to offer.

She was so serious and she watched everything with her deep black eyes. I often wondered what she was thinking as she observed us from her aloof standpoint. She didn't cry much, her method of coping was to shut down. When she did that I held her closer and whispered in her tiny ear, mama ai ni YuQing (mama loves you YuQing). Eventually she would look at me and touch my cheek. Somewhere deep inside I hoped she understood.

Over the next few days she progressed well and we tried to find a rhythm. She ate almost nonstop. She is a slow and dainty eater, but an eater just the same. She was then and she is now. You can rush her all you want but she eats at her own delicate pace.

Two hour breakfasts were our norm, which was ok with me because the coffee there was awesome! I would sip my second or third latte while I fed our little princess. Members of our travel group would come, eat breakfast and leave while we took our time. Once back to our room from breakfast (with a steamed roll in each hand) she would reach out for the bag of Gerber Puffs.

She started showing a strong preference for mom. While it was obvious she adored Serenity (Serenity even got the first kiss) Mom was the preferred caregiver. That little tidbit was put to the test when we visited her orphanage. I wasn't terribly worried about it. We visited Serenity's orphanage on her adoption trip and there was no doubt she wanted to leave with us. I felt sure Belle would be the same. It just was very important to have that closure and sense of finality for Belle. Serenity didn't want to make the 90 minutes each way van ride so she stayed back at our hotel with her new best friend Alexandria and her family.

The orphanage visit went well. It was a brand new facility, still under construction in some buildings. It was huge with multiple buildings and living situations. A few buildings were being set up as apartments for foster parents to live with three or four children in a traditional family setting.

The children had just moved there June 1. The first room we went in was Belle's. We got to meet her special 'grandma'. This was the woman that went with Belle for her hospital stays. It was her day off but she came in because she heard Yu Qing (Belle) would be there. I owe this woman so much, a debt I can never repay. How can you adequately convey the depth of gratitude you feel? This woman loved my baby. She held and comforted her when I could not. A mere 'Thank You' seemed inadequate. We took lots of pictures for waiting families and I cried plenty.

That night Belle did her first grieving session. An hour and a half of inconsolable crying and wailing is what my baby went through. There was nothing I could do to appease or comfort her. It was hard to watch but I know it had to happen. I was sure it isn't the last time we would wade thru these muddy waters.

The next day she was a happy camper. She had her first plane ride and did great. Mercifully she slept for most of it. I send out a big heartfelt thank you to the inventor of the Hip Hammock. It made going thru the airport a breeze and kept her secure on the plane while we both napped.

Our last stop on the China adoption march was Guangzhou. Guangzhou is where all Americans must visit to complete their adoptions. Here we stayed at the China Hotel. It is a Marriott property and Matt was an elite member so we had a very nice suite with executive lounge privileges. And best of all the air conditioning worked very well, something we could not say about our hotel in Zhengzhou!

To put things in perspective Henan Province (Zhengzhou) is on the same latitude line as South Carolina and we were there in July when they were having an unprecedented heat wave. Guangzhou is on the same latitude line as Havana, Cuba. We were immensely thankful for effective air conditioning!

The morning after we arrived we did a city tour. First stop was Six Banyan Buddhist temple. We missed visiting here when we adopted Serenity because she was sick. We had the option of having a blessing by a monk. We declined but enjoyed visiting and exploring the grounds

The next stop was Chen Academy. It is a beautiful place. I love looking at the traditional architecture. Funny thing was I had never thought of myself as someone who was into architecture but I guess I kind of am.

Last stop was an arts and crafts market. Ka-Ching!! We bought several goodies including tea, Belle's tea set and her baptism dress.

Once back at the hotel it was time for a nap and daddy went to do some paperwork for the consulate. After dinner we went to do a little more shopping. Belle loves the shopping. She points and babbles the whole time.

Wednesday morning we had the required medical appointment. Belle did not enjoy it but none of the kids do. Fortunately she was under two years old so she did not need blood draw for tuberculosis that all kids over 2 get.

Our last days in Guangzhou flew by. We were able to visit Shamain Island twice and it was great. I absolutely love the island. It was probably 15 degrees cooler since it is surrounded by water and tree lined. We walked around and showed Serenity some of the places that were important in her adoption trip. We shopped and had dinner at the famous Lucy's.

The consulate appointment went off without a hitch. I was able to meet the officer I had emailed with to expedite Belle's Article 5. It was so nice to put a face with the name. I thanked him for being so responsive to her need. We had left the hotel at 8:50 and were back by 11:15. It was a pretty quick trip. We did group pictures with everybody and the reality that we were heading home soon started setting in.

The next morning we had nothing we had to do except pack! After another nice two hour breakfast we started finding places for all the treasures we had gathered up along our journey. But we needed to leave a little room because the afternoon was time to hop on the bus for more shopping!

Are you sensing a theme in Guangzhou? Not only is it the place to do the American portion of the adoption but it was also the reward for surviving Zhengzhou!

We started at the Pearl Market. We bought 6 strands of pearls, 1 for me, 1 for Serenity, 1 for Belle, 1 for Nikki and 1 each to give Mattie and Donovan's brides on their wedding day, Then it was back to the island. We were able to find the shop we had been looking for and make some special purchases for back home.

That evening we bid farewell to Guangzhou and started our trip home.

As nice as a trip to China is (and it does have many high points) it is so much better to get home. With that in mind we said goodbye to our travel group and hopped in a van bound for the Guangzhou airport for our 10:30 pm flight to Hong Kong. When I was booking our flight home (on the United website)it was $200 pp cheaper to fly from GZ and change planes in Hong Kong with a 12 hour layover than to drive or take a train to Hong Kong and fly from there ON THE SAME FLIGHT!!!!

We were flying Dragon Air. Dragon Air has the coolest logo. That is where the coolness of Dragon Air ends. We got to the front of the line and checked our 3 pieces of luggage to San Francisco. Once we were finally checked in for our flight (after standing in line forever) and waded thru immigration, customs and security (oh my!) and seated somewhat comfortably on the plane, they announced a one hour delay due to traffic. So our flight left at 11:30pm instead of arriving in Hong Kong at 11:30 as scheduled. You know you are in trouble when they start serving drinks and snacks before you take off.

We arrived in HK sometime around 12:30 and were off to our last hotel of this trip, Sky City Marriott. But first we had to figure out how to get to their shuttle. We had to go through immigration and customs, even though we were still technically in China. By now it was 1 am and immigration is down to 4 officers and about 5 planes have landed. So we waited in an hour long line to clear customs and immigration from China to China.

Let me take this moment to sing the praises of sweet Serenity. She was a trooper this whole trip, even the long march home.

By the time we actually got to our hotel and into our room it was after 2 am. The three of us took quick showers and hit the sheets. We started listening to one of the several Hank the Cowdog books on my iPhone. They are wonderful for winding down your mind to help you fall asleep.

We were up and out the hotel room door by 8:30am. I am glad we booked using points because I would have hated to pay for less than 7 hours in a hotel room. We had a very nice breakfast at their buffet and were soon back on the shuttle and back to the airport.

Remember earlier when I said I booked on the United website and we checked our bags thru to San Francisco? Throw out everything you may think that means because it doesn't. When we got to the United counter to have our boarding passes printed, things kind of fell apart. But bless my sweet hubby's heart he took care of everything. We couldn't find the baggage claim tags we had received in GZ. The counter person needed them to make sure our luggage would make the plane. (???) After calling and tapping on the computer and a good bit of time, everything was hunky dory and she was able to print our passes. Let me say here and now she was a very pleasant lady and never seemed irritated at us or annoyed at the situation.

Back thru immigration, customs and security (oh my!) on a tram, down the hall to the gate and walked right on the plane. Boom, boom, boom! Now we settle in for a 12 + hour flight. I won't bore you with the agonizing details but I will say that Belle is mommy's girl and this trip was no different. She was none too pleased when I had to use the 'ladies' on the plane.

After napping and snacking for 12 hours we landed safe and sound in the good ole USA, hallelujah! We were off the plane and headed to (say it with me) immigration, customs and security (oh my!) But it was all good because Belle was a citizen!

We got in the line for immigration, choosing the US citizen line and when we came round the first bend (you know how those lines are back and forth, back and forth) there was an officer. We showed him the sacred 'do not open no matter what' brown envelope and he opened the rope and led us to a special window. The officer asked us a few questions, and directed us to 'window 40'. The officer at Window 40 gave us a form, told Matt not to fill it out and told us to have a seat until called.

There were (I think) a total of 6 adoption families on the plane. We were #2 waiting to be called. Pretty quickly we were called up to another window, bing, boom, bang we were through and on our way to customs. We picked up luggage, went thru the customs line and over to re check our luggage.

At this point we were flying standby thanks to a gift from our good friends from Serenity's adoption group that work for United. So again it took some time to figure things out. But it was all settled and looked like we could make the next flight east to Chicago instead of waiting 9 hours for a direct Pittsburgh flight. So we checked our luggage there and then it was back thru security, down the hall, round the bend, over the river and thru the woods to our gate. We waited about 15 minutes and were told, "Yes, there was room for us on this flight."

The flight from San Francisco was pretty uneventful. Truthfully, I think we must have slept the whole way because we were still on 'China time'. Landing in Chicago meant we were one step closer to home. At one point Matt said if we had to we could drive home from here.

This was the only time Belle got really fussy. And let me tell you, I do not blame her one iota! To her tiny body it is the middle of the night and she wanted to go to bed! But we made it to Chicago pretty much unscathed, waiting for the last leg of our journey.

Did someone mention LEG? Let me tell you friends, my legs were swollen up tighter than a tick. It was amazing to look at not so amazing to feel. And remember Belle loves her mommy so I was trudging with her the whole way.

So we made it to our gate for the Pittsburgh flight just as they were loading. We were 13, 14 and 15 on the standby list of a full flight. Believe it or not, one of us could have got on the flight. I was just as glad to not make that flight since the next one was only 2 hours later. I needed a break from airplanes and airplane food. So we made the trek to the next gate. Again Serenity was being a trooper, always concerned how her sister was doing. She is such a gem.

At the next gate I saw a Starbucks and gladly ponied up the dough to get Serenity and I Frappuccinos! MMMM icy goodness. Matt struck out in search of food. Successfully slaying the wild hotdog and ensnaring the cunning deep dish pizza, he ensured his family was fed.

And then I used one of our carry-ons to put my puffy tootsies up!

We made the next flight no problem and I even had an open seat beside me. We landed in Pittsburgh just after midnight making our total journey time 24 hours and 15 minutes!

Dean and Nikki picked us up and we were bound for home sweet home.

Thank You Jesus!

Chapter 7

If it's December 1941 in Casablanca,
what time is it in New York?
Rick from Casablanca

    We were finally home. Well, at least for a few
nights because we traded one suitcase for another and
drove to Philadelphia.

    Before we left for China we had made
appointments for Belle with the doctor that wrote our
expedite letter, Dr K, and her CRNP Vanessa. We had
been so blessed to find some of the best doctors and nurses
along our journey and it was exciting to meet them face to
face.

    We spent two days there having blood tests and
evaluations. We saw a cardiologist because of the tiny
hole in her heart. We saw an urologist because of her
ureter surgery in China. And last but in no way least we
were seen in the Thalassemia clinic by Dr K and Vanessa.
It was probably the longest doctor's visit I have ever been
a part of but at no time did we feel rushed or hurried. They
took their time to explain so much about thalassemia to us.
They really wanted us to be ready to walk this road with
our daughter.

    When we left we felt pretty good about our
decisions and felt we had a plan in place to care for our
baby, but an hour into our trip home that good feeling
evaporated.

    Vanessa called us and told us the result of Belle's
hemoglobin test was 7.5. She needed transfused right
away. They agreed to contact our local children's hospital
to set everything up for us.

The next day I called our local hematologist, the one that would be dealing with the main care of our daughter, Dr. Krish. Somehow, I have no idea how; I had his personal cell phone. He answered it and was so gracious to me I knew he was a keeper. He agreed she needed seen right away. So on Thursday morning, less than a week home from China, I loaded Belle into our minivan and headed for Children's Hospital of Pittsburgh.

I had only been to that hospital a few times so I relied on Siri (on the iPhone) to get me there. That was a big mistake. I got lost. I was late. I cried in the minivan as I navigated Pittsburgh's crazy streets until I found the hospital.

I was an hour late for our first appointment but I finally got to meet Kr Krish and I liked him immediately. We spoke about Belle and her limited health history. Even though I was convinced she had beta thalassemia major, he was hesitant to 'jump into the deep end of the thalassemia pool'. We had no official diagnosis at that point but all signs were pointing in that direction, I thought. I had decided to accept the worst case scenario and if I was pleasantly surprised, great.

He did a thorough exam of Belle and made extensive notes. Even though we didn't have a thalassemia diagnosis we knew her hemoglobin was low enough to warrant a transfusion so we made arrangements to come down the next day for our first clinic day.

3. That's the number of people that tried to get an IV into Belle.
7. That's the number of IV sticks Belle had that first clinic day.
7. That's the number of FAILED IV sticks Belle had that first clinic day

We had nurses try for an IV with no luck. They called the IV team to try with no luck. We were in dark rooms using the vein finder. We were in brightly lit rooms to see clearly. We used heat packs. They were all to no avail. It was a very rough day.

Her veins, like the rest of her, were very tiny and fragile. Some of the IV team put forth the theory that maybe she was more than 19 months old because her veins were so 'beat up' that she would have had more than 6 transfusions (we only knew of 6 transfusions in China for sure).

They could not get an IV but she needed blood. The next step was to have a port put in her chest to make transfusions easier, indeed possible. But this was Friday and surgery would have to wait until Monday.

Over the weekend I thought about this beautiful, beautiful child. I thought about how little I knew about her, really. She had a whole story and I only had the cliff notes . I felt a little like Rick in Casablanca when he asked Ilsa, "Who are you really, and what were you before? What did you do and what did you think? "I knew I loved her and she was learning to trust me.

It was so difficult to let them take her from me on that Monday when she went for surgery. The longest she had been away from me was the time it took to shower and I was sure her port placement would take longer than that.

Once Belle had the port in place, her monthly transfusions would be much easier. Gone would be the days of multiple sticks and a tear streaked face. It would be a 'one and done' deal.

Home less than 10 days I took sweet, little Belle to Children's Hospital to have a port put in so she would be able to receive her transfusions with a minimum of pain. Her port placement went perfectly. I was able to be with her when she fell asleep and as she was waking up. Once she was out of recovery we were sent up to a room and her first blood transfusion.

Belle started dancing halfway through that first transfusion. She kind of reminded me of Popeye eating his spinach.

We spent the night at Children's that night for a couple of reasons.

1. By the time her transfusion was over it was after 11pm and she had to be monitored for 2 hours. It would have had us leaving Pittsburgh around 1:30 am and I had been up since 6am. Matt had worked that morning so we drove separately and I didn't think I should be driving as tired as I was.

2. I was a little scared. I wasn't sure what to expect after a transfusion, this was all new to me.

My fears were unfounded and everything went off without a hitch. Belle sparked up the next morning and we were able to leave around 11 with no problems. It was time to go home and enjoy being a family.

Belle fit right into our family and home. It took a while to attach to daddy, just like Serenity. I think there are not many men around the kids in the orphanages so they just aren't sure about the male of the species.

Belle was baptized at the end of August. I love it when we have a baptism at church. And because I am a sentimental softie, I usually get weepy during them. Toddler baptisms are always a joy to witness because their reactions are priceless. Belle's baptism was no different.

After taking our place at the front of the church our pastor starts his portion. Belle was unimpressed by the solemn occasion. I was holding her, and then she wanted Daddy. No, maybe Serenity, no she wanted mommy. Maybe there would be a better view if big brother Matt was holding her. Nope she definitely wanted down. She decided she would settle for dad. Phew! Pastor Jones asked us the questions to prepare for the actual baptism and we answered them. At that point he gently cupped water in his hand and placed it on her head, baptizing her in the name of the Father (place water filled hand on her head) and the Son (more water) and the Holy Spirit (still more water).

Belle could not figure out why that seemingly nice man just dumped water on her. A few weeks later when we saw him at the church picnic she remembered and would not go near him.

I was in love and would show off my beautiful baby anywhere. We went to the local college's (daddy's alma mater) homecoming parade one sunny Saturday afternoon in October. We realized that this was Matt's 25th reunion year and his graduating class was marching in the parade. Somehow in the excitement and preoccupation with the adoption we had overlooked that. The classes celebrating their 5th or 10th year had lots of members walking in the parade pushing strollers. We were pretty sad Matt missed the chance to walk the parade with Belle. 25th reunion, 48 years old with his baby in a stroller. How cool would that have been?

Belle's transfusions were going well. At first they were every two weeks to get her hemoglobin up to a good range then they were moved out to every three weeks. The port was working great. We felt it was time to introduce Belle to a good friend, Mickey Mouse. We planned our trip for early December.

After one of her earlier transfusions the skin on the port didn't close up properly. There was a hole, presumably where the needle had been inserted, that just stayed open. It looked like a scab was holding it open so at the next transfusion I showed the nurse and she called a resident from internal radiology to look at it. He decided she could still use the port for the transfusion and they would fix it after. So after the transfusion was over the resident came back to see us and he glued it shut.

Belle was not a fan, the next morning she peeled the glue off. Back to Pittsburgh we went to have it resealed. This time the doctor gave me a couple of vials of the sticky stuff to re-glue as necessary. This went on for three more transfusions before it was decided it was too big a risk of infection to leave as it was. The port needed replaced as soon as possible. They decided this on Wednesday and we were leaving for Walt Disney World on Friday.

We went ahead with our trip and we had a great time. I knew Belle would not remember any of it, but I would and so would her dad. Walt Disney World holds a very special place in our hearts and we have been there many times but each time is special. Serenity took her first steps there and there are so many other fond memories. Belle needed to have her first trip to Disney. So off we went to spend a week in the warm Floridian sun before coming home to surgery.

December 13th, 2013 was a Friday. Friday the 13th my daughter would once again go to surgery for a port. Thankfully we were able to come home this time. Being so close to Christmas the hospital was a flurry of activity and holiday cheer. Gifts were given to kids and characters came to visit, it was a party atmosphere.

We came home Friday night ready to settle down to the Christmas season. Saturday night we decorated the tree with the whole family. Sunday we went to church and out to lunch with Matt's parents. Belle's first Christmas was in full swing!

On the way home from lunch my cell phone rang and the caller ID showed it was Children's Hospital. When the hospital calls you on a Sunday afternoon you just know it can't be good news.

They had sent Belle's old port for lab tests and it showed positive for MRSA. The caller stressed the importance of getting Belle there as soon as we could. It was time for another trip to Pittsburgh. Serenity went to her grandparents while Matt and I took Belle to the hospital emergency room. I was looking up MRSA on my smart phone the whole time and by the time we pulled into the parking garage I was on the edge of panic.

I haven't said much here about my faith but it is a very important part of our life. And sitting in that parking garage I knew that it was the most important thing to cling to. I asked Matt to pray before we got out of the car. Belle was asleep and blissfully unaware of everything going on around her. I, on the other hand, was too aware.

After several hours languishing in the emergency department and several blood tests, it was decided Belle did not have MRSA in her bloodstream. But she still needed a course of a strong antibiotic. Apparently the tip of the port's catheter, the end that goes into the vein, was the only part that 'grew' the MRSA. We never knew if it grazed her skin as it was being removed or if it was contaminated between her chest and the lab. But we could take our baby home with antibiotics and a plan for isolation during our clinic days.

Isolation meant instead of being in the big room with everyone else we were in a smaller room alone. It had its good points and its bad points but we did just fine. Belle needed nasal swabs for a few months to prove she was MRSA clear before we could go back to the big room.

Friday the 13th was her port surgery; Friday December 20 was her birthday. Her second birthday but her first birthday at home with us. And as I said before it was also my baby sister's birthday what a great reason to have a big family party. We had so much to celebrate, life was feeling pretty good.

After the birthday celebrations it was time for Christmas celebrations. Serenity went with my mother to see Santa Claus. When they came home my mother shared with me what Serenity told Santa. She told Santa the only thing she wanted for Christmas was her family all together and happy. That is a deep wish for a ten year old. I called her brothers to tell them and we all decided to make it happen.

Christmas that year was terrific. Nothing livens up the holidays like having a new baby, especially if that new baby is 2 years old. We were all together and it is safe to say we were all happy.

After the wonder and magic of Christmas comes the dark days. You may know them as January, February, March and April. We call them tax season.

Matt is a CPA and partner in an accounting firm. The first four months of the year he works lots of hours. Between 10 and 12 hours a day, 6 days a week make up his work schedule. Normally I work in his office 40 or more hours a week. This year we had decided since we had Belle I would only work 2 days a week.

So I spent Tuesdays and Saturdays at work with Matt and Belle spent the day at her grandparents. I missed her. She missed me. But it was only for a few months and then life could go back to normal.
Or so we thought.

Chapter 8

How can there be too many children? That is like saying there are too many flowers. — Mother Teresa

"So are you done?" I get that question every so often. It seems everyone has an opinion on family size, especially someone else's family size. Most people are more than happy to share their opinion with you.

When I'm asked that question my answer is,

"I've been done 3 times."

We were done after the twins. 3 boys in 2 years equaled tired, stressed parents.

We were **DONE!**

We were done after Serenity. We finally had a daughter, our family was complete.

We were **DONE!**

We were done after Belle. We were getting older and this would be it for us.

We were **DONE!**

And then it happened. Like I have said before I belong to a Facebook group for parents that have adopted children with thalassemia. Part of the mission of the group is to advocate for waiting children. One day on the group I saw an absolutely beautiful baby girl just a few months younger than Belle. Her listing name was Rose. She tugged at my already fragile heartstrings. I showed her picture to Matt who gave me the go ahead. I contacted the agency that had her file and got a copy to review. I forwarded the file to our Pittsburgh hematologist's nurse practitioner and the nurse practitioner from Philadelphia.

The collective verdict was beta thalassemia major, just like Belle.

We put our name on the list to be considered to adopt her, all the while praying for the right thing to happen. Since we were within 12 months of our last adoption we could reuse large portions of our dossier. We asked if the agency she was listed with would transfer her file to our agency so we could reuse. If she was meant to be our daughter I knew it would all work out. I'm going to admit here and now that her age kind of scared me. Belle kept me moving and let's faces it, I wasn't getting any younger!

Before I really had time to worry about it another wonderful family already with that agency submitted a Letter of Intent. Rose became Lainey and I had the privilege of following her parent's journey to adopt her and became friends with her mom via our Facebook group.

Rose/Lainey was God's way of paving the path for our next big journey.

Soon another sad little face was staring at me from my computer monitor. She was listed with the same agency Rose had been. Her listing name was Olivia and she was 6 years old.

Now I have never been accused of being a math whiz but even I could figure out that 6 fit quite nicely between 10(Serenity) and 2(Belle). Once again after consulting with Matt, I called the agency and requested a copy of her file. The agency sent me a copy but told me her file was currently on hold for another family. Once again I forwarded the file to my 'Thalassemia Team' and waited. Olivia did indeed have thalassemia but she had a different type. She had Alpha Thalassemia, specifically Hemoglobin H disease with Constant Springs mutation and a very enlarged spleen.

This is where things get kind of confusing. I think the following events were definitely a God thing.

On the Facebook group was another mom who had adopted a son with thalassemia at exactly the same time we adopted Belle, right down to the day. She had fallen in love with a little girl listed with the same agency way back in November, she was known as Allison. Because this mom's last adoption was through a different agency she was also requesting a transfer of the file so she could reuse her dossier. She kept getting pushed to the bottom of the list for this little girl in favor of families already signed up with the agency. Family after family put Allison on hold and took weeks to say no and release her file. The mom kept in contact with the agency with great hope of adopting her and she saw Olivia's picture too. When she called to ask about Olivia, the agency sent her the file and put Olivia on hold for her family.

This mom and I chatted back and forth and I assured her I just really wanted Olivia in a family. She didn't belong in an orphanage, she needed a family. Olivia knew what 'family' was because she had been with her biological family until she was 5 years old.

This was all transpiring in February during the thick of tax season. My friend and I continued to discuss and hash out our feelings while caring for the two children we had with thalassemia. She had decided she was going to switch to the agency that held the two girls' files since it seemed like they were unwilling to transfer the files for reuse of our dossiers. Since it appeared that Allison was not going to be available, my friend was going to pursue Olivia.

Then it all started happening. Allison became available to my friend! She messaged me with great excitement and encouraged me to fill out the lengthy online application because she was releasing Olivia's file and I was next on the list.

Matt did the bravest thing he has ever done. While I felt really good about her age, he was nervous that she was already 6 years old and concerned about the level of heartbreak she must have endured being abandoned at 5. The effects of grief and trauma are very real and they can be scary. But he is a good man with a good heart, and he believes in the power of love and family. I felt a strong calling by God to move forward and he said he'd been praying. Then he said that he trusted me, if it was weighing so heavily on my heart then we would do it.

When I called the agency to tell them we wanted to move forward for Olivia I also inquired if any other families had expressed an interest. There was one other family. I asked how far along they were in the process. The social worker was not sure so I told the social worker if the other family was farther along in the process and could get Olivia home sooner we would step aside for them. This surprised the social worker and she said she would get back to me. The following Monday when she called me back she asked me why I would be willing to let the other family adopt Olivia. I explained to her that Olivia needed a family and medical treatment as soon as possible and that waiting for treatment could cause some serious problems down the line. She told me she had been praying over the weekend that we were Olivia's family because only a true mother would put the child's needs before her own, even if that meant losing the child. The other family was just in the very beginning stages and didn't have a homestudy or any of their dossier done.

We were Olivia's family.

I have often thought about the statement of the social worker, "only a true mother would put the child's needs before her own even if that meant losing the child". When I think of that, I think of my daughters' birth mothers. Serenity was around 3 months when she went to the orphanage and Belle was around 9 months. Betty June (Olivia) was 5 years old. Read that again, 5 years old, when she went to the orphanage. "Only a true mother would put the child's needs before her own even if that meant losing the child."

Chapter 9
Don't fight a battle if you don't gain anything by winning.
Erwin Rommel

March 1st Matt and I started the process to bring our third daughter home. March seemed like a perfect time to once again start paperchasing for an adoption. I mean there was nothing else going on, like say, tax season or corporate filing deadlines. But Matt and I are a good team and we work really well together. We knew we could make this happen.

Our dossier was pretty up to date and even though we could not technically re-use it we could recycle it! Most of the forms were on either his or my computer and it only took a little tweaking to make them up to date. I had a network in place to get letters for expedite and it just took a simple visit from home study social worker to do an update.

Oh wait, did I say simple? Nothing, I mean, nothing about this adoption was simple.

Let's start with the home study update. Because we have a well instead of city water we had to have our water tested, again. Let's set aside the fact that we have all been cooking with and drinking this water for 20 years with no problems and concentrate on the fact that you cannot drink the water in China without boiling it. But that was really just a small annoyance compared to USCIS fiasco.

I was impatient; I know that. I wanted everything done as quickly as possible. We needed to send in a few things to USCIS to be able to adopt another child on the original certificate. So I asked my assigned agency social worker if I could send in all the required forms myself once we had the home study update in hand. I wanted to save the step of mailing her the hard copy. She said yes once she reviewed the update our local social worker had emailed her. A few days later she said she reviewed it and I mailed it to USCIS.

After last year's terrible officer, I had been transferred to an angel of an USCIS officer. I emailed her Olivia's file and the expedite letters, she took them to her supervisor and got permission to expedite our case. She gave me terrific instructions on what I needed to do to make things move smoothly.

She found the mistake.

Our homestudy update was incomplete and the paperwork was missing a letter from the agency. She called me and told me what she needed. I called my agency social worker and left a message. I then emailed the social worker. The social worker emailed me back and said to let her know when I got it straightened out.

And that is when my head exploded.

I never knew people actually saw red when they got angry, but they do, I saw it for myself.

When we did the 'orientation interview' with this new agency they told us they were very proud of being a 'hand holding' agency. I felt this omission was a major oversight. Not to bring money into this but we pay these agencies a pretty hefty fee to guide us through this complicated process. The homestudy update should have been reviewed more thoroughly by our agency social worker. Our local social worker should have been given some guidance by the agency. For Belle's adoption less than a year ago that agency sent a template for our local worker to follow.

Have you ever heard the expression "the squeaky wheel gets the grease"? I was squeaking quite loudly.

But this little girl was meant to be our daughter. And like another old expression, "If God brings you to it, He will bring you through it", we found the way through it. In the thalassemia Facebook group one of the mom's is a social worker for this agency. She took our homestudy, made it correct, sent it to our local worker and made it all work out.

Knowing we had a thalassemia mom working with us gave great relief to us.

So on April 23 I took the required letter from the agency, the corrected homestudy update and a copy of the original homestudy to the post office to overnight it all to USCIS.

Once we received the USCIS approval our dossier was ready to go thru two more steps to be completed.

Anything with a signature in your dossier must be notarized. This includes the homestudy signed by the social worker, medical forms signed by your doctor, your financial statement signed by you, petition to adopt also signed by you, etc. The whole dossier, approximately 13 items, then must be certified. That means after a dossier document has been notarized, it must be "certified" by the Secretary of State where the Notary Public is registered. That verifies that the Notary whose name appears on the document is indeed a legal Notary in that state by attaching a certification page to each document.

Once you receive the dossier back from the state, you get to repackage it for 'authentication'. After a document has been certified by the Secretary of State, it must be "authenticated" by the Chinese Consulate. The Consulates will verify the authenticity of the Secretary of State's signature.

Our dossier was finally ready to go to China. It was logged into their system on June 10th. We had completed a new dossier in just 3 months. The next big step was the Letter of Acceptance, also called the Letter Seeking Confirmation. The wait from LID to LOA was now running somewhere around 90 days. Once again we were trying to expedite the China portion of the adoption but this time we were having little luck. This agency felt they knew the 'right' way to handle it. But their way was very ineffective to put in the nicest way possible.

The director of the China program set up a conference call with the mom adopting Rose, the mom adopting Allison and myself to try to better understand thalassemia. We spend some time explaining what thalassemia was, and why it was so important to get these kids home for treatment. We told her about the ongoing blood shortage in China and the importance of proper chelation. She seemed eager to get this information into the hands of the orphanage directors and medical personnel in China. Because of the difficulty of translating medical terminology into Mandarin she asked if we had any resources. I really want to believe the best about the agency's motives and sincerity but I have been left with serious doubts. Plus it seemed pretty arrogant for us as Americans, especially American laypeople, to tell Chinese doctors how to treat thalassemia.

In the mean time life at our house continued on as the clock ticked. The last week of May we once again headed east to Philadelphia to visit CHOP. June brought the last day of school for Serenity and summer activities which we always enjoy.

The last weekend in June, Matt, the girls and I traveled to Chicago to attend the Cooley's Anemia Foundation Patient and Family Conference. That conference was incredible. It was such a blessing and encouragement to meet adults living with thalassemia and other families that have a child with thalassemia. We learned so much and came away with such renewed hope for Belle that I was recharged to fight for 'Olivia'.

I was able to speak with a nurse practitioner from Children's Hospital of Oakland about getting the information about thalassemia already translated into Mandarin. Oakland has a larger than average Asian patient base so they already had what I needed. I was able to forward those resources to the China Director at the agency so she could get them into the hands of orphanage directors and staff.

Chapter 10
The dandelions and buttercups gild all the lawn: the drowsy bee stumbles among the clover tops, and summer sweetens all to me. - James Russell Lowell

After the Cooley's Anemia conference came my favorite month of the year, July.

Our family has a lot to celebrate so July becomes one long party.

1.   4th of July. Usually Matt and my brother-in-law, Ron, have a booth at a local festival. Since they have gotten older our son, Dean, is running it but that doesn't stop Dad and 'Unc' from helping out. I try to keep a low profile during that little event.

2.   Serenity's adoption anniversary is July 5th. This year marked 10 years of Serenity being in our family. We always try to make it a special family day. This year we took an old time train ride to celebrate.

3.   July 9th, Dean and Nikki's anniversary. We are so blessed to have Nikki in our lives. She is a very important member of our family and we just have to celebrate their day.

4.   Serenity's adoption group reunion. Last year it was at the beach and we were getting ready to go to China to bring home Belle. This year it was in Gatlinburg and we were waiting for Betty June (Olivia). Bonus feature: My cousin from Kentucky was visiting Gatlinburg at the same time so we got to spend an afternoon with him.

Double bonus: on the way home we got to have lunch with a little boy and his mom from Belle's travel group!

5.   July 20th Serenity's birthday. Her brother, Mattie, got her Just Dance 4. Cake, ice cream and dancing were the highlights of the family gathering. Happy 11th Birthday, Serenity!

6.   July 26th Poppy's Birthday. Matt's dad turned 78. He declined dancing but said yes to ice cream cake!

7.   July 26th our wedding anniversary. That is not a typo. We were married on my father-in-law's 50th birthday. I tell him I was his birthday present; he asks me what the winner got!

8.   July 29th Belle's 1st adoption anniversary. We kept it low-key this year because she is still young and really doesn't understand the meaning of this day. Family dinner and fun time to celebrate.

July also meant we were 31 days closer to Betty June. Allison's mom and I were in almost constant contact. We felt like two allies in the trenches fighting our way to China for our kids. We felt like our agency wasn't totally supporting our efforts to bring home these two sick little girls quickly. We watched several people successfully expedite the process with other agencies. We saw families with later log in dates receive letters of acceptance before us; each one was a dagger to our heart.

July was an emotional roller coaster. But soon it was August.

Chapter 11

What's in a name? That which we call a rose by any other name would smell as sweet.

William Shakespeare

Naming your child is one of the best parts of the adoption process. I say that because at that point, holding a picture and calling the child by name is a very uplifting moment. Actually naming your child during pregnancy is an equally special time. The child stops being an abstract idea and becomes real.

All of our children have meaningful names.

Matthew Clark is our first born child. We had so much fun choosing his name. We didn't know if he was going to be a girl or boy until he was born. If he was a girl he was going to be Erin Margaret, Margaret after Matt's mother. Up until two weeks before he was born we had Jan Matthew chosen for a boy. One of Matt's favorite musical groups is Jan and Dean, so Jan had a strong position. We both really thought it was going to be a boy so that is where our focus was. The pregnancy went two weeks overdue and we started second guessing ourselves, maybe Jan wasn't the direction we wanted to go. So we dropped Jan and went with Matthew as a first name. Matt's favorite baseball team is the San Francisco Giants and their first baseman was Will Clark. Hence Matthew Clark, we call him Mattie.

Our twins are Dean Mark and Donovan James. Because of the twin pregnancy, I had numerous ultrasounds and we knew they were going to be boys. Mark was chosen for Matt's brother that died of childhood leukemia, we really wanted to honor his memory. Matt's dad is Donald and my dad is James but Matt's dad didn't really like his name growing up and thinks everyone needs their own name. I really liked the name Donovan so it was an easy change and still honored him. And Dean? Well, between Jan and Dean and Dean being a character on one of the TV shows I watched regularly, it was an easy fit. Dean Mark and Donovan James were chosen.

Serenity Mareline Jean FuZhu is a great story. Matt and I had a hard time deciding about adoption at first. It was a struggle. I started praying for peace for our decision. I asked God to either clear a path or take away the desire. When we decided to adopt a daughter from China one of the first things we did was tell our boys. After telling them, Dean says, "We can name her Serenity!" The sun shone down on us and I think I heard angels singing because all along I had been praying for peace. I had been praying for serenity. When we received her referral over a year later we found out her Chinese name, Fu Zhu means peaceful blessing. And I am sure you noticed she has several middle names. At the time I thought I was getting only one daughter so I wanted to use all the names I liked. Mareline (pronounced mar-leen) is my middle name and it is a family name. My aunt's middle name is Mareline, and my great aunt is Mareline so I wanted to continue it. Jean is my grandfather's wife. She married a man with two children and her favorite expression was "the only steps in my house lead to the cellar" She had no stepchildren, no step-grandchildren she only had kids and grandkids. She taught me family is much more than blood, so I wanted to honor her. Serenity Mareline Jean FuZhu Dailey does all that and more.

Isabelle Margaret Agnes YuQing, I thought, was my bonus baby. She is named after four great women.

Isabelle is my mother's mother AND Matt's mother's mother. Margaret is Matt's mother. Agnes was my father's mother that I lived with until she died when I was 11. We call her Belle and she truly is a beauty.

Now we get to name 'Olivia'. And while Olivia is a perfectly good name it just didn't 'sing' for us. I have told you Matt's older brother Mark died of childhood leukemia when Matt was 6. Matt's parents spent lots of time taking Mark to doctors and hospitals and Matt spent a lot of time at his dad's sister's house during that time. Aunt Betty took care of Matt. She taught him to play games and became a very important person to him. It was an easy choice to name our next daughter Betty June after her. Dareline is my sister Ramie's middle name. Yes, our names rhyme Jamie Mareline and Ramie Dareline, it's a southern thing (my parents actually went through the alphabet to find a name that rhythms with Jamie) and Liu Ling was her Chinese name.

Her name became Betty June Dareline LiuLing Dailey.

Chapter 12

Patience and perseverance have a magical effect before which difficulties disappear and obstacles vanish.   John Quincy Adams

Betty June's birthday is August 24th. It had become painfully obvious that I wasn't going to make it to China for her 7th birthday.

My goal had been to be with her for her birthday, but that was just my goal. When it became obvious that wasn't going to happen we arranged with Helen (one of our agency's reps in China) to send her a birthday party. Helen sent us some pictures from the party and a video. That may have been a mistake. Birthdays are not a big deal in China and she looked pretty overwhelmed. Earlier in the process we had sent her a photo album full of pictures of us. In the pictures Helen sent us of her party Betty-June was looking through the album.

August is the month of our annual beach vacation. Every year we spend a week on Long Beach Island at Harvey Cedars Bible Conference. We really enjoy our time there and we had missed it last year because we were just getting home from China. This year the travelers were Matt, Serenity, Belle, Mattie, Matt's mom, dad and me.

We always take two days to drive there and with a two year old it made sense to break up the trip as much as possible. We stopped for a nice lunch at a favorite pizza place in Centre Hall then went to the chocolate factory in Hershey before spending the night in a hotel and continuing out to LBI.

I was getting a little antsy because I knew we were getting close to LOA. I was checking email and Facebook several times a day. It was pretty obvious I was on the edge because Mattie suggested he and I go out for a fun night. The local theater group was doing 'Spamalot'. He and I share a love of musical theater so off we went on Wednesday night to laugh our cares away.

Thursday we got LOA. Our dossier was logged into China's system June 10th and it was now August 14th. It had been a 65 day wait, more than twice the wait for Belle's. The agency emailed us a copy of the LOA. We went to the reception desk at the bible conference since we had made arrangements to use their printer. They were able to print it for us. We signed it and the staff scanned it and sent it straight back to the agency. We also forwarded a copy to our USCIS officer to await their next step, issuing the I-800.

19 hours.

That is what it took to get USCIS approval to call Liu Ling (Betty-June) our next of kin (that is basically what the I800 form is). Last year it took 2 weeks. What was different this year? This year we had an officer that knew her job, she knew what she could and could not do. AND SHE DID IT! I thank God (literally) that our paths crossed. I felt like I should have sent her a fruit basket or something.

August 25th I filled out our daughter-to-be's visa application. For the first time I was officially declaring her Betty-June Dareline LiuLing Dailey. That felt really good. Because I am a total sentimental fool this is how I thought of it: August 24th Liu Ling celebrated her birthday, August 25th she was reborn as Betty-June.

Chapter 13
Busy, busy, busy
~~~Professor Hinkle from Frosty the Snowman

Our small town still starts school the Tuesday after Labor Day, this year September 2nd. Serenity started middle school this year. She was so excited, but Belle was not happy to see her go off to school every day, neither was our dog, neither was I. I like having my kids home with me. I am kind of a mother hen that way; I like all my little chicks under my wing. Add that to the fact that one of my little chicks was half way across the world and you will get my state of mind.

But the day took a turn for the better because our Travel Approval showed up in the online system. Nothing could really happen until our agency received the actual piece of paper in their hands but it was on its way.

To celebrate Matt took Belle and me out for Chinese food for lunch. At the end of the meal we all crack open fortune cookies and my fortune reads, "You shall seek out new adventures." Poetic?

Our agency had requested the travel approval be emailed to them but were told it could not be done. This was very disconcerting to us because we were pushing up against a major Chinese holiday, National Day. The American Consulate would be closed from Oct 1-5, so no appointments those days and Chinese offices are closed Oct 1-8 so nothing can happen then. I was told the only days we could get our consulate appointment are Sept 22, 25 or 29 because the 23 and 24th are full.

Oh the drama, oh the angst! I was so worried travel would get pushed back another month. If I didn't get an appointment on one of those days I wouldn't get to meet her until Oct 13. But our agency person told me to go ahead and contact a travel agent because when it happened it would happen fast. I talked to a very nice agent, discussed routes and he gave me instructions on what to do when I found out my consulate appointment.

So I went to bed Wednesday night, September 4, with all this on my heart and mind. While I was sleeping someone in China decided they COULD email the travel approval. Thank you, whoever you are.

Our agency was able to secure us a September 22 consulate appointment meaning I could meet Betty-June Sept 15. I was flying to China on Sept 11.

On Sept 6th I had a party at my house. Every year our local adoption group celebrates a few Chinese holidays together and in the fall that holiday is Moon Festival. The best way to describe Moon Festival is to compare it to our Thanksgiving, it's not the same thing but that is the best way for Americans to understand it. We invited our friends over and had a big potluck dinner. It is so good to have friends that understand the adoption journey. It is a huge source of support and comfort.

Planning for my trip was hot and heavy at this point. I say my trip because this time I was going alone. We had decided that Matt should stay home with the girls this time for a couple of reasons.

1. Finances. One could travel much cheaper than four and since this was our second adoption in less than a year that was a concern.

2. Belle's health. Because Belle has a port we have to be very diligent about fevers and such. If she gets a fever it means a trip to the emergency room. Also if she gets sick her hemoglobin drops faster than normal, potentially meaning the need for a transfusion. Neither of those

things would be good if we were in China when they happened.

So I was going to be a lone traveler. Not going to lie, I was more than a little nervous going without Matt; he's my best friend and co-conspirator. I knew I was going to miss him and the kids like crazy. But one of my kids was in China and needed me to come get her. So what's a mommy going to do but go?

Chapter 14
Don't Panic.
— The Hitchhiker's Guide to the Galaxy

September 11th I left Pittsburgh International Airport at 8 pm. Kissing my family goodbye at security was possibly the hardest thing I had ever had to do. It was going to be a 25 hour trip to get to Betty-June's city. I would get to Guangzhou, China at 9am Saturday morning (9pm Friday night EST) that is right folks, for the 4th time in my life I got to experience the miracle of time travel! Seriously though, what an age we live in that we can travel halfway around the world in only 25 hours! The plane from Chicago flew for 15 hours to Hong Kong WITHOUT STOPPING!

But I am getting ahead of myself. My flights were pretty uneventful. My flight from Pittsburgh was 45 min late leaving but I had a 4 hour wait in Chicago for my flight to Hong Kong so if I sat in Pittsburgh or Chicago didn't matter to me.

When I finally got to Chicago I was pretty proud of myself for navigating the huge airport even changing terminals all by myself. I grabbed a bottle of coffee from a shop and settled in at the gate waiting for my long flight to China. As I was checking out Facebook I saw that someone had posted on a friend's wall that they had made it to the gate for their flight. I looked up and saw a couple sitting across from me. I took a chance and said, "Are you the Browns?"

They were! Instant friends! We started chatting when we were joined by another young man, Nathan, who was traveling to help his sister on her adoption trip. Finally, friends of the Browns joined us; The Powells too were traveling to Guangzhou for their adoption. Turns out their daughter has thalassemia also.

The waiting time for our flight flew by because all of the sudden I had 'community'. When we boarded our flight it was only half full. Nathan and I shared a row with an empty seat between us. We felt like we had it pretty good. After takeoff we had a light dinner and settled in for the long haul. We were spread out nicely. The flight attendant came thru and asked if we were together. When we told her we weren't she told Nathan there was an empty row he could have. When he moved I had 3 seats to myself. I was able to stretch out to sleep. That was a huge luxury on a 15 hour flight. A little sleep aid, a little TV, I passed the time quite nicely.

Landing in Hong Kong I knew I was that much closer to my daughter. Again, I've got to pat myself on the back for navigating thru another huge, and this time foreign, airport all by myself. I bought a Coke, found my gate, called my hubby, told him how much I miss him and the kids and ran into the Powells again. I found out they were on the same flight to Guangzhou because their daughter was also from Guangdong province.
It was a quick flight to Guangzhou. I made it thru immigration with no issues, collected my luggage and found my guide. Guess who had the same guide? Yep, the Powells! Turns out our agencies shared a guide.

So now I knew Brian and Heather Powell from Illinois were in my travel group. Heather is a nurse and Brian is a minister. The fact that Brian is a minister is no small thing because I have never, ever adopted from China without a minister in my travel group. First trip was Jason, Baptist minister from Mississippi. Second trip was Chad, Baptist minister from Michigan, and now Brian, Nazarene minister from Illinois. Tangible proof to me that God went with me on all these trips, very comforting.

The hotel I stayed at was very upscale. The guide helped us check in and I got settled into my room. I had a two room suite with a sitting room, bedroom and gorgeous, over the top bathroom. All of that was lost on me at the time because I was homesick. I missed Matt, I missed the girls, I missed my sons and I had a bad case of the 'poor-me's. I was being absolutely ridiculous! I spent the day in my room watching TV, napping, and unpacking.

I was traveling alone and we weren't sure how our new daughter would adjust. I seemed like a wise choice to pay the additional fee for me to have executive lounge access. I could have dinner every night in the executive lounge and not have to venture out with a child that may be having a really hard time. I had read about older children not wanting to stay with the new parents and trying to run away. Being in a country where I couldn't communicate very well made me a little more cautious. If Matt had been with me we would have tried a new restaurant every night and really soaked it all in but I was a woman traveling alone to a strange city adopting an older child so it seemed more prudent this way.

So when evening came I went up to the executive lounge for dinner and it was extremely nice. I gave the hostess my best 'Ni Hao' and showed her my room card. I never had to show it again, they remembered me and greeted me by name each time thereafter. Cool stuff.

The next morning I was up at 3:30am to face another day alone in Guangzhou. Jetlag was not my friend. So I watched some international TV. My favorite became a Korean soap opera called 'What Happens to My Family'. It was odd but I really looked forward to watching it in the coming days. Before I went to breakfast I was able to video call my family. That was awesome. I missed them so much. It was confirmed to me that I am not a loner!

Hotel breakfasts on China adoption trips are completely awesome. Quite possibly they are the best meal of the day. You have a choice of Asian traditional breakfast offerings of congee, dumplings and noodles or Western breakfast offerings of eggs, bacon, and sausage or both. I chatted with a few other Americans in the buffet line but ate alone.

Even I could recognize I was getting pathetic. It was time to leave the hotel. For one thing I needed fresh air since I hadn't left the hotel since I got there and, more importantly, I needed to find a supermarket to get a few things. I was meeting my daughter tomorrow!

I was able to navigate the busy streets and find a grocery store all by myself! I felt pretty proud of myself, and, truth be told, just a little smug. That may not seem like a big deal since the store was just across the street but it was. In order to cross the street it involved going down to the subway and going UNDER the street and finding the way out without being able to read the signs. Yep I did it, yea me! I was there 20 min before the mall with the store in it opened so I sat in the square to wait. People watching!

We hear a great deal about China's growing gender imbalance in the adoption community. Culturally sons have long been preferred. After the institution of the one child policy that became problematic to poorer families that for one reason or another need a son. That attitude is changing in China, slowly but surely it is changing. I thought I would conduct my own very unscientific study on the issue. By way of gender imbalance, while waiting, I saw 5 boys, 4 girls and 2 infant I couldn't tell the gender.

Finally the mall opened and I was forced to abandon my research. I headed up to the 4th floor where the groceries were. I wandered and perused the offerings. I wasn't sure what to get Betty-June for snacks and goodies. I had picked up a few things including snacks for myself but I wasn't sure what a 7 year old Chinese girl would really like. I found a family with a 7ish year old girl and tried to notice what she asked for. If she asked for it, I picked one up hoping she had good taste!

My oldest son, Mattie was very concerned about my safety traveling alone. Outside the mall was a mobile police station so I took a picture of it and sent it to him. On Belle's adoption trip Serenity and her dad made daily trips to the 7-11 for drinks and snacks. There was one right outside the mall so I took a selfie in front of it and sent it to them. With my iPhone I was able to have them with me, in some small way I wasn't alone.

I spent the rest of the afternoon in my hotel room. I arranged and re-arranged trying to prepare for Betty June. Fortunately the HBO was in English and I watched movies while drinking good jasmine tea acquired on my shopping trip. At dinner time I went back to the executive lounge and was greeted by name. I had my last dinner alone.

The next day was Betty-June Day! September 15th was finally here and once again I woke up at 3:30 am. I made myself tea, bought during the previous day's adventure, and watched some more Korean soap operas until breakfast.

I was able to have breakfast with an online friend. She was adopting a 6 year old with thalassemia and was a member of the Facebook group. It was so nice to have a sister with me. Like me she was alone for this part of her trip because her husband was meeting their other child in his province, they were adopting two boys. Her husband was in a city I was very familiar with, Zhengzhou where I met Belle. She and I talked and talked over breakfast like old friends, and we were going to meet our kids together.

Meeting your new child at 3 pm is cruel. All day you fret and pace and you are expected to be able to fill out official paperwork. Time dragged until it was time to leave the hotel. I gathered up all the paperwork I would need, a backpack of goodies and a Minnie Mouse plush to give Betty June when we met.

The ride to the Civil Affairs office was excruciating. Would she like me? Could I communicate with her? Did she even want to leave China? I was a wreck.

When we got to Civil Affairs she was there waiting for me. I had tears running down my face like crazy when we first met. There she was right in front of me. She was a beautiful stoic princess. She was understandably very afraid. I was this big, fat American woman crying like mad. It took a while but she did eventually smile. I gave her the backpack and the Minnie Mouse I had brought her. She was wearing the shoes and hat we had sent to her and she had a backpack with our photo album in it. I spoke to her thru our guide. She finally smiled and began to relax. It was pretty perfect.

I also got to witness my new friend, Amber, meet her son as well as the rest of my group including the Powells meeting their daughter. That day 3 Chinese children with thalassemia were welcomed into their new families. It was pretty special.

After all the excitement we came back to the hotel and went for Chinese food with the Powells. Their new daughter was 13 and I say she was born to be royal because she really took care of us that night. When we Americans were struggling with chopsticks she asked for forks. She got us more napkins and drinks; she was a princess hosting a royal feast. Betty-June and I had our first meal together.

We tried to call Dad after dinner but the video chat wouldn't work because something was wrong with the hotel wifi. That really bothered me. I missed the folks at home, I wanted to share everything with them and I wanted the sisters to meet each other.

Our first night together went off without a hitch. Each of us slept in our own bed and I only woke up a few times to check on her. I wanted to make sure I hadn't dreamed it, she was really with me.

Just before breakfast the next morning somehow the video chat started working. I felt so happy to be able to talk to my family at home. Betty June got to 'meet' them too.

We went to breakfast as a duo. I let her pick out what she wanted and she chose salted fish and peanut congee. She scraped the bowl clean and we went back for more. She loved that stuff.

After breakfast we went back to our room for an hour to play. Play-doh was a big hit. We spent hours during the rest of the trip sculpting with it.

That day was the official adoption appointment. What a looooong morning. I don't remember it taking so long with Belle but it must have. While waiting I met a couple from France and a couple from Australia adopting babies. It was really interesting to hear how their process is different and similar to ours.

As part of officially adopting her I sat across the desk from a Chinese official. He asked me a series of questions just like the other two adoptions. "Why do I wish to adopt a Chinese Child?" "Was I aware of her medical needs?"Etc. But this time I was alone so he asked why my husband was not with me and did he consent to this adoption. It is important to note that as part of preparing for our trip I had to get a Power of Attorney from Matt notarized, certified and authenticated to complete this adoption. I told the officer that Matt had not traveled with me so he could stay home and care for our other two daughters; I also threw in the fact that they were also adopted from China. I explained that like Betty June, our daughter Belle had thalassemia and we felt she should stay home and not make the long journey. Since she joined our family so recently we didn't want to both leave her so I came alone. I think I may have given him too much information because he started chuckling. He said, "Daddy tell you, "Go bring me beautiful Chinese daughter!"" And with that he stamped our paperwork and Betty June was ours.

Once we finally left the official appointments we stopped at the market again for some supplies. This time Betty June was able to show me what she liked. She picked out some instant noodles and milk drink. She also chose a beautiful dress with pink roses, the frilliest and laciest dress we saw and Hello Kitty sneakers. My girl was a shopper!

Some families in our group were going to McDonald's for lunch but we were dragging. The 12 hour time difference kicks my butt and I had been waking up between 3 and 4 am. We came back to the room and made instant noodles for lunch, which were terrific. Betty June introduced me to some Chinese kiddie shows. I may have taken a nap too.

Monday we met, Tuesday I adopted her in the eyes of the Chinese government. The next day was the required medical appointment. Since our group spent the whole adoption trip in Guangzhou we could have our appointment midweek instead of Saturday like families that had to go to other parts of China to meet their children. Because of that our visit was pretty low key, there weren't many others there. Betty June got to play with her new friend Wen Cai another 7 year old girl in our group.

Everything started off just fine. She had her vitals taken. There was a quick eye and vision check. It was like any other physical.

The visit got scary for me when we were taken into the next room; we got to the part where they do the actual physical examination. The younger female doctor started out just fine until she got to Betty-June's abdomen and her enlarged spleen. She got a very serious look on her face and went for the older male doctor. He checked her belly and asked me when her last transfusion was. I had asked the nanny that accompanied Betty June to our first meeting and was unhappy with the answer. When I told him Aug 4 his face went dark and he told me she needs a transfusion every month. Yes, I was semi scolded by this man because Betty June had up to this point been transfused every 10 weeks and she needed it more often. (UMMM no kidding Doc, how bout let's pass that on to the rest of the country and get these adoptions sped up!) He wanted her hemoglobin checked and thought she would need a transfusion before we left China.

One of the reasons it is so important to expedite an adoption of a child with thalassemia is the chronic blood shortage there, especially in south China where we were. Blood is not always available and when it is they may not receive the full amount. That is just how it is. The hospital where Betty June received her transfusions required a 3-4 day stay in the pediatric intensive care ward for her treatment. And the worst part is, I could not go with her or stay with her. Now throw on top of that, this is the very hospital she had been abandoned at less than 2 years ago. I was expected to send her there for 3 days alone. How much damage would that cause to our fragile bonding and her little heart?

It was a long night while I waited to find out her hgb. It was impossible to get a straight answer from our at home medical team regarding how low is too low to travel. IMPOSSIBLE.

I struggled to balance what she may need physically with what I knew she needed emotionally. Matt and I spent most of that night (day back home) texting each other. We were both emailing doctors trying to balance her needs.

The next day her hemoglobin level came back at 6, not great by anyone's standard. But good enough I felt I could say no thanks to transfusing her in China. Sad but true, she had been living with low hemoglobin, so 6 for her was not as serious then as it would be now that she is getting transfused more often.

I felt a lot better after we decided that. I was able to keep her with me instead of leaving her alone at a hospital.

Sept 19th we were able to visit Betty-June's FORMER orphanage.

It was hard. From the moment my sweet girl woke up her countenance was downcast. All morning she was sad.

Betty-June chose to wear the new dress she picked out at the mall. I know she was afraid I was going to leave her. I guess she wanted to make sure she at least had her new dress. I used the translator app to tell her I was going to take her to my home to be my daughter forever, but she wasn't convinced. She hadn't learned to trust me yet. It had only been a few days and sure it had been fun and the food was good but I guess she thought maybe it was too good to be true.

We met Miko, our guide at 1 o'clock for the 45 minute ride. Miko tried to explain to her that I wasn't going to leave her. She would be coming back with me, I would never leave her. Baby girl fell asleep in the van on the way there.

When we arrived, I woke her up she was still sad and unsure. We went in and did the usual 'go to the conference room exchange pleasantries and exchange gifts'. They were very kind. The director thanked me many times for adopting 'Ling' telling me she was the sickest child they had.

(I want to add here that the method this adoption agency used for expedite was to ask the orphanage director to contact the CCCWA to expedite the adoption, specifically the LOA. This director thanked me profusely for adopting 'Ling' not once but many times. It caused me to wonder if she had ever been asked to help speed the adoption along. Because of protocol I could not ask her.)

Betty June's teacher brought in her workbooks for her to take with her. One nanny brought in a little girl I was checking on for her mom-to-be. Then we went to see some important places to Betty-June, school room, play room, playground. Along the way we met her two best friends. She just clung to me the whole time unwilling to let me out of her sight, in case she was left, and unwilling to share me.

One of her best friends, a boy, pleaded with me to find a family for him. He is seven and he has a repaired cleft lip and palate. His speech is affected but his mind is sharp. He was in several of the pictures I had received of her. He really, really wants a mama and baba. He also said he is a good big brother (guhguh). Break my heart much?

Eventually I got to meet 2 of their newest additions, both with thalassemia, a boy and a girl. The director said they were preparing their paperwork to make them available for adoption. I tried to encourage the director to finish their paperwork as soon as possible because younger children get chosen faster.
When it was time to go Betty-June could not leave fast enough. I dare say she never looked back.

It was a hard day, a very hard day. If you can walk thru an orphanage and hear the little voices begging, begging I tell you, for a family and not be moved; you, my friend, have no heart.

After the visit I felt we had turned a corner. Up until then I had been calling her Ling to ease her transition, but after that day I wasn't calling her Ling any more. She was no longer Liu Ling the orphan. I had started calling her Betty-June Ling, easing into just Betty-June.

We finally left the orphanage, none too soon for my daughter. Betty June fell asleep again almost immediately. It should have taken between 45 min and an hour to get back to the hotel. The most important word in that sentence is SHOULD.

We got lost.

Miko and the driver were both using their cell phone navigation to try to find the way back. I got to see old Huadu village, and by old Huadu village I mean narrow, narrow alleyways. We were in a minivan. The alleys were 1 minivan and 6 inches wide. We were lost for over an hour. We did more u turns than a dozen games of Scrabble. And Betty-June slept the whole time! Good times, good times. But we did drive by the hospital where Betty June received her transfusions.

That was Thursday, Friday morning we went to the Guangdong museum in the morning. It was ok but Betty-June tired pretty easy so we took our time walking through it. At the end of the trip before getting back on the bus she and I decided to find a bathroom. Hello Squatty, my old nemesis! Betty June, like her big sister, expressed much dismay when faced with a squatty potty and she had lived in China her whole life!

Saturday she and I went to Shamain Island and did some shopping. The rest of our group was either going to the zoo or safari park but I was concerned about Betty June's stamina. On Shamain we could take our time and leave when we needed too.

So a cab to Shamain Island it was! Chinese taxi cabs are really fun. And by really fun I mean 'OH MY GOSH, ARE YOU FREAKING INSANE?' It's not just a drive; it's a near death experience. But visiting 'The Island' is worth it. We wandered in and out of little shops, bought some presents for ourselves and people at home.

We found a small jade bracelet for Betty June. Since I wear two jade bracelets all the time I thought she might like to wear one also, to make her feel special.

Shamain Island has some pretty famous (at least in the adoption community) statues. It is something of a tradition to take pictures with the statues and finally I had a child that would cooperate and liked having her picture taken. While we were strolling around the island we passed the Catholic Church. Outside the church is a life sized statue of Jesus and the little children. Betty June ran up to the statue and wanted her picture taken. And I was reminded that 'Jesus loves the little children, all the children of the world...'

The next afternoon brought more paperwork. Want to feel stupid? Answer this question:
What is the correct way to write the date?
A) September 19, 2014
B) 9/19/14
C) 19/9/14
D) 19/SEP/2014

The answer is: it depends.

No matter which way you write it there is a 75% chance you are wrong, such was my adventure in filling out more paperwork. Each form needed a different format. On our other adoption trips Matt handled this part and I got to stay in the room and play with the baby. But this time I am here solo so I get to enjoy/endure this part too. Another facet of it just being her and I, Betty-June gets to go with me to these paperwork parties. Fortunately she is an angel and more patient than I deserved.

Since these children are leaving their homeland most parents like to find treasures to give their children special to China. For girls pearls and jade are two of the most popular choices. The guides know this and arrange shopping trips accordingly. September 20th we visited the pearl and jade market to make such purchases. At the pearl market I bought a string of pearls for Betty June for her wedding day. I also found gorgeous lavender colored pearls, true color not dyed, for both grandmothers for Christmas. After buying the pearls we went on to the jade market. Betty June needed a jade bracelet like her sisters.

The girl working at the counter commented on the fact I was wearing two jade bracelets already. When the guide told her this was my third Chinese daughter quite a bit of chatter erupted behind the counter. They thought I was either crazy or wonderful; I was wise enough not to ask for a translation. We picked out a bracelet for Betty June and we were off to the next stop, Chen Ancestral Hall.

We had been there a year earlier and knew there were treasures to be found there. Betty June found a stuffed panda she wanted, and I wasn't saying no. I also found a beautiful tea set to give her when she is an adult, something we also did for Serenity and Belle.

The morning of September 22 something happened besides shopping, a very important step, our consulate appointment. My girl was dressed in red, white and blue for this monumental occasion. The appointment itself is a tad anticlimactic. About 50 parents crowd around an officer behind a window and take an oath. Then we are called up one by one give them our paperwork folder, then go back to the first window and get fingerprinted again. Then you leave. That's it. No flag waving, no Star-Spangled Banner, no John Phillips Sousa, not even any John Denver.

Most days Betty-June and I ate dinner in the executive lounge. The menu was on an iPad complete with pictures. Technically they were heavy appetizers but it was easy to make a meal of them. Betty June, like her sisters, loves soup. So every night she had soup along with whatever else we chose. I found out that she preferred water over soda. However, in China I have found my absolute favorite soda I have ever had, Watson's Ginger Ale. By the end of our trip I had a nice little stockpile in our room refrigerator because every evening I took one or two back with me.

Lunch, we usually had in our room. The room had an electric tea kettle to boil water because remember you cannot drink the water or even use it to brush your teeth without first boiling it. We would use the boiling water to make instant noodles. Our hotel room became our little refuge from the hustle, bustle and heat of China.

Breakfast was probably our favorite meal of the day. Besides the awesome assortment of food it was a major social time. There were plenty of families staying there that were adopting. Our own group has swelled in numbers as we were joined by families with children from Chongqing coming to Guangzhou to complete their adoption. Nathan and his sister as well as the Brown family were back with us. After breakfast we fed bread to the fish in the large goldfish pond. Our life together had found a nice routine.

That evening, our last night in China, she and I went on the Pearl River Cruise with our group. It was my first time doing that and it was quite an experience. The food was very authentic. Some of it was really good. We had ice cream for dessert and it was purple. One of the other moms and I made a game of guessing the flavor. Sweet potato? Corn? Turns out it was taro. Close enough.

After dinner we went to the observation deck to watch the city go by. It was all lit up with neon and looked its finest for us. Betty June spun around and around. She seemed so happy.

On the way home from the cruise the guide explained to Betty June that tomorrow we were going to America. That is when the other shoe dropped.

Up until that point Betty June was getting happier and livelier every day but that night was our first real grieving session.

She tried to hide from me in our room. She crouched behind the curtains. She made herself as small as she could in the corner beside the bed. I tried to get her to come to bed. She had started sleeping in the same bed as me after our trip to the orphanage but now she wanted nothing to do with it. When I tried to hold her she started wailing and she wailed for 2 hours.

She was sad, she was angry. She had a hundred questions coursing thru her 7 year old mind. My daughter's heart was breaking and I couldn't even comfort her. She finally cried herself to sleep lying next to me.

Adopting a 7 year old was a lot different than adopting a baby. Her fear and sorrow was so real, so palpable, it blanketed the whole experience. She was losing everything she had ever known. I, a stranger, was asking her to trust me, to let me love her, to come with me to a new country, to learn a new language, to be part of a different culture. I was asking her to let go of everyone and everything she had ever known and loved for an uncertain future. I was promising her a better life; she just had to believe me. Does that sound familiar? If you are a Christian it should.

Chapter 15

You know how advice is.
You only want it if it agrees with what
you wanted to do anyway.
John Steinbeck

After 4 adoption trips to China, I came up with a letter I wanted to write to every parent going to China to adopt.

Dear Chinese Adoptive Parent,

While in China, I give you permission to:

1. Eat junk food you never would at home.

Maybe you are vegan/paleo/whole food/low carb/insert way of eating here. When you are in China it is ok to hide out in your hotel room scarfing down Pringles and Twinkies. They call it comfort food for a reason.

2. Watch TV shows you would never (admit to) watch at home.

If it is in English and makes you less stressed go for it. Eating cup 'o noodles for lunch while watching Korean soap operas with English subtitles is ok.

3. Overpay for souvenirs.

Sometimes you can bargain, sometimes not. I, personally, am not very good at bargaining. I try, get a little discount and both the merchant and I feel like we won. Plus how often will we be in China? I need that (insert tacky item here).

4. Think China is wonderful/weird, probably at the same time.

She call it foreign for a reason. Just remember they are older and bigger than us so please behave.

5. Overpay for convenience.

Upgrade to a bigger hotel room? Pay for executive lounge privileges? Whatever it takes to get you through, is ok.

6. Not wear makeup.

At home maybe you never leave your house without your face on but on your adoption trip it is full on survival mode. You will never see most of these people again and the rest of the people in your travel group are too jet lagged/busy gazing at their new child to notice.

7. Use or pass up a squatty potty.

I promise you we all feel the same way about them. There is no judgment either way.

8. Take food from the breakfast buffet for later.

Yes, that is a banana in my pocket.

9. Ask stupid questions.

We were all wondering the same thing probably.

10. Talk to strangers in elevators.

If you get on an elevator and see a Caucasian family with an Asian baby it is perfectly acceptable, née even expected, to make small or not so small talk. You have joined a very special fraternity enjoy it.

11. Think you got the best kid in China.

You'd be wrong because I got the best 3 in the whole country but go ahead and think that.

Chapter 16
Airplane travel is nature's way of making you look like your passport photo.
Al Gore

The next morning we left the hotel at 5:30 am. We had arranged for a van to take us from Guangzhou to Hong Kong.

Betty June gets one of her middle names from my sister. We tease my sister about having car-calepsy. That is if Ramie is a passenger in a moving vehicle she falls asleep, almost always. Up to this point Betty June has shown signs of possible having the same 'syndrome'. Unless we are on the bus with other kids she falls asleep. I had high hopes the trip to Hong Kong would be no different.

From our hotel to the airport would take 3ish hours then we caught a flight just before noon (midnight at home) for Chicago, go thru customs and immigration and then on to Pittsburgh. Once we landed in Chicago, Betty-June was no longer a citizen of China but an American citizen. And Hallelujah, we would be almost home!

The van trip to Hong Kong was actually pretty pleasant. For one thing the van was sleek, shiny and practically brand new, for another Betty June fell asleep.

The driver put a video in for us to watch on the long trip. It was Mr. Bean. My family loves Mr. Bean so I felt that much closer to being home. Crossing from mainland China into Hong Kong requires going through a check point much like going from the US into Canada. They examined our passports and took our temperatures.

We made it to the airport and I was on my own. We found where to check in for our flight. We checked our luggage, got our boarding passes and headed through security. Once on the other side I saw a Disney Store. I just had to go in; I am a bona fide Disney freak so really I had no choice. I bought Betty June a Toy Story play set and a copy of the number one movie for little girls at the time, Frozen. The movie was in both English and Mandarin so Betty June could enjoy it even before she knew English. By now we were hungry so we had our last meal in China, dumplings and soup, while she broke out the Toy Story figures.

We found our gate but it was roped off. I wasn't sure why but there was a large group of people sitting around that seemed to be waiting for the gate to open, so we joined them. It turned out that all flights to the US and Australia was requiring a second security check. When the gate opened we lined up to go through security again, US citizens in one line and all others in a different line. When Betty June and I got up to the security officer to show our passports the young man insisted Betty June and I be separated and she needed to go through the other line because she had a Chinese passport. I kept insisting she stay with me. I tried showing him her adoption decree and telling him she was my daughter. He was completely unimpressed and would not budge, neither would I. Finally his supervisor came over to see why the line was not moving. She was 5 ft nothing and seemed tough as nails. Realizing she was in charge, I showed her the adoption decree and said the Chinese word for daughter (at least I hope I was saying daughter).She must have been a mother because once she figured out what was going on she waved Betty June and I on and gave the young officer quite a chewing out! Our carry-ons were quickly inspected and we were free to go.

Our flight to the United States was 15 hours long. Betty June's very first time on an airplane was a 15 hour trip. Unlike my trip to China, this time the plane was full. My girl was a champ on the trip. She never complained. After our night before I was concerned maybe she would put up a fuss getting on the plane but she was happy and joyful the whole time. She had decided to trust me.

Landing in Chicago meant she was now an American citizen. However, unlike our immigration experience in San Francisco last summer, Chicago's was a long, unpleasant experience. We had almost 4 hours from the time we landed in Chicago to the time our plane left for Pittsburgh. That should have been enough time to gather our luggage, go thru customs and immigration and get on our plane with no problem. But somehow we got caught up in immigration with a refugee group. Finally the immigration official gave us back our passports and jotted down Betty June's case number on her visa without completing everything.

I was very close to emotionally falling apart. An airline worker whose job it was to help you recheck your luggage by telling you which line to get into recognized my fragile state. He took our suitcases from me, promised to get them checked for us, wrote down our gate number and told me everything would be ok. He said we would make the plane (he would call to have it held for us) but our luggage may not make it on that plane. I didn't care, I wanted to go home. We barely made our plane to Pittsburgh. I think we may have been the last two people on the plane, if not we were close.

We finally landed in the Steel City. I was so happy I could have kissed the statue of Franco Harris. As Betty June and I rode the escalator down to baggage claim I saw my husband and daughters waiting for us. I unashamedly burst into tears. All the nerves, all the tension, everything I had been holding in for two weeks came cascading down my face in a big ugly cry. Once I was able to contain it I introduced Betty June to her new family all with tears streaming down my face.

The airline worker had been right. Our luggage did not make it onto the plane with us but it was on the next one and would be in Pittsburgh in 90 minutes. We took that time to let Betty June get to know her sisters and dad. I was so relieved to be back with them. And she seemed pretty happy to get to meet them in person after Skyping with them.

We were home. But our real journey had just begun.

Chapter 17
Home is where the heart is.
Pliny the Elder

They say 'A journey of a thousand miles begins with a single step.' Maybe so but it ends with sleeping in your own bed.

Before I left for China we were in the process of finishing Betty June's new room. While I was gone Matt was going to finish painting it, assemble the new bed, hang the new Minnie Mouse curtains and make the bed with the new Minnie Mouse bed set. While I was in China Betty June showed a strong preference for Hello Kitty. A quick call home and Matt was able to exchange the Minnie Mouse for Hello Kitty. When we got home she and I both got to see her new bedroom for the first time.

That night it was so nice to sleep in my bed with my husband and baby. Betty June declined to sleep alone, even though she loved her room and instead chose to bunk with her new big sister.

Knowing that her hemoglobin was very low, the next afternoon we made the first of many trips to Children's Hospital of Pittsburgh. Since she was not established as a patient yet, we were told to go in through the Emergency Department. The staff really jumped to it when we told them that, "Yes, we had been out of the country in the last three weeks. As a matter of fact we just got home from China LAST NIGHT." This was right at the beginning of the Ebola scare so that little tidbit of information got everyone's attention.

Betty June's hemoglobin had dropped to 5.5 since her medical appointment in China so we were admitted for an overnight stay and immediate transfusion. Betty June's stay and transfusion were uneventful. Since she is a little bigger than Belle she was able to have an IV with minimum trouble. Matt and I spent the night with her and were able to take her home the next day with a plan to bring her back in two weeks when her sister, Belle, was scheduled for a transfusion. It is so amazing to see the change that blood can make. Before the transfusion she was pale, jaundiced and somewhat sullen (maybe it was fear of the unknown) but after the transfusion she had pinked up, the jaundice in her eyes was gone and she was back to the giggly girl I had known in China. She skipped down the hallway leaving the hospital ready to meet her new life head on!

Chapter 18

Never go to a doctor whose office plants have died.
Erma Bombeck

When adopting a special needs child, especially a child with a chronic or ongoing condition, you bring some pretty important people into your life, your child's medical team.

When Belle came home our first doctor visit was to Children's Hospital of Philadelphia to see Dr K and her nurse practitioner, Vanessa. They had written a letter for us to help expedite Belle's adoption. Dr K is the head of the thalassemia clinic. She was able to point us in the right direction with Belle's care.

At our home hospital, Children's Hospital of Pittsburgh, we were fortunate enough to be seen by Dr Krish. We felt he was a terrific doctor and he seemed to understand her needs. When I was concerned about the amount of blood ordered for Belle by the nurse practitioner, that it wasn't enough, he agreed saying, "We don't need to make these kids beg for blood." He told me to never consider a bone marrow transplant for Belle since we didn't have a biological donor available to us, and that we should wait for gene therapy. Bone marrow transplants are his specialty so I trusted that he knew what he was talking about.

When I told him we were pursuing a second daughter with thalassemia he enthusiastically reviewed her file for us. He told me of his trips back to India to work in clinics and seeing families with thalassemic children and the stigma it carries there. He took a great deal of time to explain about the different types of thalassemia, how thalassemia started and its relationship to malaria. There are so many nuances to the disease and he seemed to know them all, I could have spent hours just listening to him. But since he was so good and outstanding in his field of Bone Marrow Transplantation, Pittsburgh could not keep him and he moved on to bigger pastures.

Belle was randomly assigned to Dr C. She seemed like a nice enough doctor and since thalassemia is so rare in our area I had no expectation she would be an expert.

Since we were going in through the emergency department with Betty June, she got assigned the hematologist on call, Dr M., again a very nice doctor with limited thalassemia experience.

It was inconvenient to have two different hematologist for our family but we figured we would take a 'wait and see' approach, knowing we would know the right hematologist for our family when the time came.

Also as the result of Dr Krish leaving there was a shuffling in the pediatric hematology/oncology department. We would no longer see the nurse practitioner we had grown accustom to seeing, now we would see a bright young physician's assistant, Michael. Belle and Betty June refer to him as 'My Michael'. They simply adore him. When we get to the hospital after they get checked in and vitals taken we walk down the hall to the infusion clinic. If 'My Michael' is in the hall they race to him to give him dual hugs. 'My Michael' has spent a great deal of time fine tuning his thalassemia knowledge which I greatly appreciate. He is happy to reach out to Children's Hospital of Philadelphia's Thalassemia Clinic when he needs to get more guidance. He designed a spreadsheet to track the girls' treatment to make sure there is no annual testing we miss. He even read the Standards of Care when he was on vacation with his wife.

My girls have no fears or misgivings about going to the hospital for their blood transfusions because in their minds it is a big play date. The nurses in the clinic are a big part of the reason they feel this way. Mindy, Eileen, Marilyn, Rose, Nikki are just a few of the nurses that make their visits pleasant. When they see their nurses for the first time of the day there are more hugs to give out. They aren't big fans of IVs or port accesses but it is a small price to pay (in their minds) for the good times that follow!

Like most kids here in America, the girls also have their primary care physician, Dr Ben. Matt and I grew up with Dr. Ben. Matt has known him since they were little kids attending Sunday School together. Dr Ben married a woman that was adopted as an infant from Korea. So while international adoption medicine isn't his specialty, he does have a special interest and heart for it. I like to tease him that if he doesn't return my calls fast enough I will call his mom. You have to love those small town connections.

We are very fortunate to have the medical team we do. Each one of them plays an important part in the lives of my girls. From the woman that gives us our day badges at the front desk of the hospital, to the triage team, to the blood bank staff all the way to the nurses and doctors, each link in the care chain works together to keep Belle and Betty June healthy.

Chapter 19

Life is really simple, but we insist on making it complicated.
Confucius

I still remember the Christmas when I was 5. The family had awoken early and opened our presents around the tree. My grandmother and mom went into the kitchen and started making a big farm breakfast and my dad turned on the TV while I played with my new baby doll. I got the shock of my life when Scooby- Doo came on the screen. Christmas was on Saturday that year. It had never occurred to me that holidays happened on a day of the week. I thought they had their own day, Thursday, Friday, Christmas, Saturday, etc. (In my defense I was only 5). When we have major life events we expect the world to stop for a while so we can soak it in and enjoy it, much like I expected Christmas to have a day outside the days of the week. But we all know that doesn't happen. We came home from the hospital with Betty June and life just kept marching on and it was our job to keep up.

Betty June had joined our family at the beginning of party season. Most of the family has birthdays in the autumn, throw in holidays like Halloween, Thanksgiving and Christmas and you have one long party season. Adding to all the parties were the doctor's appointments and hospital visits and the schedule just got crazy.

Serenity stepped into the role of mother hen. Like Mattie that personifies the role of Big Brother to the World, she has adopted Big Sister as her role in the family. She is bossy and demanding of her little sisters but she is also loving and gentle. If she is nagging them about brushing their teeth it is only because she doesn't want them to get cavities. Someday she will be a wonderful and very organized mother!

Belle was thrilled to have another big sister and Betty June stepped into the role almost perfectly. For a little girl that just weeks before only spoke Mandarin and a tiny tot of 2 just learning to speak, the communication often took funny turns. Bows are fashion necessities for our little girls and choosing the bow of the day is a hallowed ritual. One morning in early October Belle and Betty-June were discussing/choosing hair bows. I think they were speaking English. It could have been Chinese. It sounded like Martian. Bows got chosen and I had a good chuckle. Welcome to the new normal.

There was a big family dinner for Matt's birthday and it was Betty June's first experience to have our whole clan together. All three brothers, three sisters, one sister in law, two grandmothers and a grandfather gathered around a birthday feast was probably a little overwhelming for her, but she was so excited it was hard to tell. She once again chose the dress we bought on our first morning together in China to wear, the one covered with pink roses and lace.

Those early days were spent cuddling in my chair flanked by Belle and Betty June while big sister, Serenity, went to middle school and daddy went to work. We watched a lot of cartoons and kiddie shows in those days. Belle and Betty June were both learning to speak English so they were sponges.

Betty June continued to have grieving sessions. Matt got to see his first session right after we got home from the first hospital visit, two hours of weeping, wailing and being angry. I think sometimes her poor little brain just got overtired. It had to work so hard in those early days and everything was so strange to her.

Big brother, Mattie, got to witness an epic grieving session for himself on a weekend getaway.

It was a gorgeous autumn in western Pennsylvania, topping it off, we finally had all three of our girls at home with us along with two of our sons. To celebrate we did a weekend getaway at a local indoor waterpark with the girls and brother, Mattie. We had a really nice two bedroom suite at the attached hotel that included a kitchenette and living area with sofa bed. One bedroom had a king size bed and ensuite that Dad and I shared with Belle. The other bedroom had two double beds, one for Serenity and Betty-June and the other for Mattie with an attached bathroom.

We had spent the morning at the waterpark and true to Team Dailey form, came back for an afternoon nap. We went back to the waterpark for the evening. Everyone seemed to be having a good time and no one really wanted to go back to the room and see the fun end so we pushed it too far and the dark clouds rolled into Betty June's eyes.

Once I realized what was about to happen I alerted Matt and we hustled everyone back to the room. Betty June started crying and wailing in a big way. About 90 minutes into the expected 2 hours I took her into her bedroom and laid her in bed. I told her we would be in the living room if she needed us. I left the door open and sat at the table with Matt and we started playing cards, well within sight of Betty June.

Protective big brother did not approve of our method and let us know in no uncertain terms. He loved Betty June and hearing her heartbreak broke his tender heart. Betty June wasn't crazy about him yet but he loved her deeply already. We were all tired from activity and stressed from dealing with the fallout and we snapped. Mattie yelled at us, I yelled back, he and I were toe to toe yelling at each other when we noticed Betty June had stopped crying. I guess seeing us lose it snapped her out of her grief cycle. She came out to us, sat with me and cuddled until our pizza was delivered.

It became very important for me to remember my daughters are more than just 'my girls' they are also Chinese. A fact that I knew but, truthfully, I didn't think about much until now. All three were born in China and came to us at different times in their lives. Serenity was 11 months old. Belle was 19 month old. They were just babies and as a result are ethnically Chinese but culturally American.

Betty-June was 7. For 7 years she lived in China and China was all she knew. She is both ethnically AND culturally Chinese even though she is an American citizen. What does that mean? It means things are easier for everyone if I keep that in mind and let that be part of OUR lives. It means learning to make congee so she can have something familiar for breakfast or lunch. It means finding Pleasant Goat on YouTube for her. And it means cutting her a lot of slack when she gets out of sorts because everything is so different.

As time goes on she has become more culturally in line with us and we have become more in line with her. She wasn't the only one changing. All the girls were counting in Chinese and English and Chinese words peppered our conversations. All three girls, along with mom and dad, love Chinese dumplings, and even have them for breakfast and Belle is happy to laugh along to Pleasant Goat.

Halloween was the first American holiday she got to experience. We participated in our town's festivities in a group costume. We were Gru, Lucy and the three girls from Despicable Me 2. Betty June wasn't sure why we were doing something so crazy but the promise of candy kept her going. We took third place in the group costume division.

After Daddy's birthday came Dean and Donovan's birthday followed by Grandma, Mattie then Mommy's birthdays. December brings my dad's birthday, my grandmother's, my sister's and Belle's birthday all before Christmas!

Thanksgiving in our family, like most families, is a huge day of feasting and celebrating. My mother in law makes turkey and all the trimmings and I make ham and mashed sweet potatoes. In the eyes of Belle and Betty June, ham wins, no question. It was so much fun to watch them sneak back to the buffet table and grab another piece of ham, then another, then another.

When Christmas came Betty June smiled for three days straight! She wasn't sure about this Santa Claus fellow, neither was Belle. It all seemed a little strange to them but as long as he came through with the presents they would let the weirdness slide.

But before Christmas we had to get through December 1-24.

Chapter 20

Maybe Christmas, the Grinch thought, doesn't come from a store.
Dr. Seuss

Oh, December. It is the only winter month that warms my heart. For the rest of winter I am more Grinch than I probably should be. But December, oh sweet, sweet December, How I do love you.....Usually
This December was a crazy, frantic month for Team Dailey. Let me give you the quick tour.

Dec 3-5 Philadelphia for semi- annual visit to CHOP and Philadelphia. This was Betty June's first visit to the Thalassemia Clinic. Both girls were seen by Dr K and her team. So we drove 6 hours each way. After spending the morning at the hospital we took the girls to the Please Touch museum. We also visited Chinatown that evening for dinner. You know you are in for a great meal when you enter the restaurant and you are the only non-Asians there. One of our waitresses was from Guangzhou like Betty June. We got lots of extra attention and the staff all came over to say hello to the girls. Belle was happy to smile and wave. Betty June wasn't interested. They tried to speak to her in Mandarin but she just shook her head. We say she is shy in two languages

Dec 9 Betty June had 13 baby teeth taken out, 2 permanent teeth crowned and 2 permanent teeth filled. When just surviving is a struggle, dental care is way down on the list of need-tos, as a result Betty June came home with some serious dental issues. We had to be at Children's at 6:30 for her 8 AM surgery under general anesthesia but because of hgb issues and low platelet count due to an enlarged spleen they wanted standby blood. If you've ever had general anesthesia you know that you must be fasting beforehand, so Betty June had not had anything to eat since the night before. It takes time to get appropriate blood from the blood bank so we had to wait through a type and cross test and wait for the blood. She went into surgery at 2. We got home at 7.

Dec 10 Surgical consult about Betty June's enlarged spleen. She had an abdominal scan earlier and the results were that her spleen was severely enlarged (which we knew). The big decision was if she needed it removed or could she keep it. Removing it trades one set of issues for another so the decision was made to try to shrink it with frequent transfusions. That way even if she needed it removed it would be a much simpler procedure.

Dec 12 Matt and I dental checkup (no cavities)

Dec 14 Put up Christmas tree with the whole family. All the boys and Nikki were there to help put up Betty June's first Christmas tree. Again she wasn't sure about why we brought this big tree into the house and now we were hanging do-dads and what-nots on it but she sure thought it was fun! Brother Dean lifted Serenity onto his shoulders to put the angel on top to finish it off.

Dec 15 Transfusions in Pittsburgh, for Betty June at least. Belle's hgb was 10.1 so Dr C would not transfuse her. Apparently she had just been to a conference and decided she was concerned about iron overload from too many transfusions. This mommy was less than happy. I will cover this incident later in the book, but this was the incident that showed us which hematologist would take care of both girls.

Dec 16 Belle and Betty June audiology appointments back at Children's, part of the yearly screening regimen.

Dec 17 Betty June echocardiogram back at Children's, more of the yearly screening regimen.

Dec 18 My grandmother's birthday so the little girls and I went to see her and have cake with my mom and aunt. This is the grandmother that Belle is named after.

Dec 19 Serenity's play. Big sister attends a weekly drama class which she loves. The whole family turned out to see her Christmas production.

Dec 20 McFadden Christmas party in town, my grandmother, Isabelle's family. The girls sang three songs at the party, Jingle Bells, Jesus Loves Me and Mama Hao. That's a pretty big accomplishment for Betty June, (only speaking English for 3 months) and Belle (just 3 years old) and long suffering, big sister Serenity.
AND it was Belle's 3rd birthday and my sister's 43rd birthday so after the family Christmas party there was cake and ice cream at our house.

Dec 22 Belle and Betty June pediatrician appt with 2 immunizations each and Betty June got to visit her school classroom in anticipation of starting after the first of the year! She was supposed to go back the next day for their Christmas party but....

Dec 23 BACK TO CHILDREN'S for the blood transfusion Belle should have got a week ago. Her hgb was 9.1 and she had experienced a miserable week. But when we got to the hospital the girls were each given a HUGE gift bag full of gifts. There were at least 10 Barbie dolls in the two bags. Betty June's had an Elsa dress (from Frozen for those of you hiding from pop culture) Belle's had a 'Frozen" ukulele and small Elsa doll. There were slippers and puzzles; they each got a baby doll and too many gifts to list. It was both overwhelming and humbling at the same time.

Dec 24 Christmas Eve at my house for 16. When the boys were little Christmas Eve meant 'The Cousins Show' my kids and my sister's kids would put on a play or variety show for the adults. It was my favorite Christmas tradition. I miss those shows because apparently when you get into your 20s you are too old for that. Next year we will start The Sisters Show! But it was still a good time that included games and prizes. I was so happy Dean and his wife came late in the evening and spent the night to be here Christmas morning. And we were able to get our annual 'Girls only, matching jammies' picture. Another Christmas tradition started when Nikki joined our family is all the girls (at the time Serenity, Nikki and I) get matching Christmas pajamas and, of course, there must be pictures!

Dec 25 Christmas Day at my house for 12. Same son and his wife made Christmas breakfast for us. It was awesome!

Dec 26 I DID NOT LEAVE MY BEDROOM!!! I am totally serious. Matt took care of the little girls and I just hung out and watched TV played FB games and de stressed. I slept through breakfast but hubby brought me lunch and dinner. By the next day I felt like I could face the world again.

As a result of our 'busy with life stuff' December I didn't have time to get overwhelmed by Christmas preparation. I still had too many cookies and fudge for the holiday, and we had our silly games on Christmas Eve with scratch off lotto prizes (that I sent son, Mattie, to buy on Christmas Eve day and he had to go to 3 gas stations to find one that still had Christmas themed lottery tickets) and it's not like anyone suffered from lack of food over the holiday. Christmas Eve and Day I was actually present in the moment instead of fretting about the next thing to come. I wouldn't recommend that particular method to enjoy Christmas but it is what happened this year.

Chapter 21

If you aren't fired with enthusiasm, you
will be fired with enthusiasm.
Vince Lombardi

Back to December 15th's transfusion day.

Some may think I overreacted to Dr C's decision
to not transfuse Belle when her hgb level was at 10.1 when
traditional thinking is to transfuse when it drops below 10.
However, anyone that is living with thalassemia knows
there are many different factors to consider. For instance,
how hydrated is the person when their hemoglobin level is
tested? A well hydrated person will have a lower level
than a dehydrated person. The difference between a 10.1
and a 9.9 is pretty slim.

Belle's first hemoglobin level to be above 10 was
on May 15, 2014, it was 10.1 on that day and she was
transfused. Three weeks later on June 5 her level was 10.4
and she was transfused. This pattern continued all the way
through to August when it was decided that maybe she
was at a place now that her transfusions could be every 4
weeks instead of 3 weeks (coincidentally the second
transfusion the new hematologist, Dr C, was overseeing).
September 16 and four weeks between transfusions she
was at 10.1 and transfused.

October 13, her first transfusion with her sister,
Belle's hgb was back down to 9.3 at 4 weeks out. It was
decided to once again bring her transfusions back to three
weeks coinciding with Betty June's.

Each time previously Belle's hgb had been over
10, Dr Krish had still chosen to transfuse her but adjusted
the amount of blood she received, because remember, his

philosophy was, "We don't need to make these kids beg for blood."

And let's address iron overload. That was Dr C's big concern with giving Belle blood that day.

Because of so many transfusions there is an unavoidable build up of iron in her body. That sounds weird doesn't it? Someone with chronic anemia has too much iron in their body. No matter how odd that sounds, it is true. The iron level is measured with a blood test and it is called 'ferritin'. So before every transfusion, when she is getting blood drawn for hgb level and type and cross, they also draw blood to measure her ferritin. Once a child is over two years old and has a ferritin level over 1000 twice in a row they start on a chelation medication. So Belle started taking a daily medication to get rid of the excess iron in February 2014. It is called Exjade.

Every morning before we have breakfast I dissolve a big white pill into Belle's liquid of choice and she drinks it down. We add more liquid to redistribute the remaining residue and she drinks that. We do this EVERY SINGLE DAY! And guess what. It is working. Belle's ferritin level is steadily trending down.

Another tool to measure iron overload is a special MRI called a ferriscan. The normal range would be measured at 0.17-1.8. Belle's first ferriscan was in May 2014 and her result was 8.6. After taking Exjade almost 18 months she had another scan in June 2015. This time the result was a significant drop to 3.5. For Belle, Exjade works.

Combating iron overload will be a part of both these girls' lives until there is a cure for thalassemia. We cannot avoid this but we can fight it.

Now let's talk about quality of life. Belle deserves to feel as good as possible. She is a sweet little girl that is happy 95% of the time. As she gets more anemic she starts feeling less and less her usual happy self. She is too young to really understand what is happening in her body or express herself. So she cries. And that was how she spent the weekend of her third birthday.

On December 15th when 'My Michael' told me that Dr C would not change her mind about transfusing Belle, I told him I had decided which hematologist we would choose to treat both girls and it was not Dr C. The paperwork to change was started that day. He told me I may receive a call from the head of Hem/Onc to discuss our decision. That call never came; I think they knew why we made our choice. Both girls now had the same hematologist.

Chapter 22

Education is what remains after one has forgotten what one has learned in school.
Albert Einstein

By Christmas Betty June had been home for 3 months and by all accounts was doing beautifully. The grieving sessions were happening less and were shorter. She seemed to be settled into our family and attaching well to all of us. It appeared to be time for her next adventure. SCHOOL!

We visited the school in mid December with her but had been in contact with the school since May about her. After many conversations with the wonderful principal, Mrs. Martin, it was decided that Betty June would finish the school year with second grade then repeat second grade the next year with the same teacher.

Many factors went into deciding this. In our school district kindergarten and first grade are in one building, second through fifth in another, sixth through eighth is in a middle school, then high school is ninth through twelfth. If Betty June finished the school year with first grade she would just get used to a building and system then have to change. By staying in the same building we felt it would build her confidence. She would be spending most of the day with an English Second Language (ESL) teacher anyways to get her caught up. She had never attended school in China so she had lots of catching up to do academically. By finishing the year this way it was felt she would be ready to face second grade almost full time in the fall.

Is it perfect? No. Betty June has had to miss field trips, class parties and other fun stuff because of her transfusion schedule. But she has learned so much in such a short amount of time. And truthfully, things are never perfect, period. Life has a way to tossing us curve balls in the best of situations.

I can't say enough good things about the support and encouragement our small town school district has given us. Betty June misses at least one day of school every three weeks for blood transfusions. They happily work around her needs. Due to her enlarged spleen she needs a modified gym class. Her gym teacher exchanged emails with 'My Michael' until they had a good program worked out for her. Her ESL teacher seems wholeheartedly invested in Betty June's success. No parent could ask for more from their school district, and as a former homeschool mom, I am a tough sell.

Chapter 23

"It's the biggest pain I've ever experienced, I love it and I can't recommend it more highly."~~Brad Pitt on adoption and fatherhood

"What would you say to a family considering adopting a child with Thalassemia?"

Do it!

There has been some talk lately online about what one needs to consider when adopting a child with thalassemia. I wanted to sit down and think long and hard about that.

How prepared was I when I saw Belle's picture for the first time and fell head over heels totally and unequivocally in love with her?

What is 'Not At All', Alex?

I did all my searching and learning AFTER we decided to adopt her. I Facebooked, I Googled, I Yahooed, I even Binged in an effort to educate myself. I called, emailed and texted to reach out to others who knew more than me. I lead with my heart and let everything else fall into place. I got lucky. I live an hour from an awesome Children's hospital and 6 hours from a Thalassemia Center.

For those of you who lead with your head and want to know how to be prepared I wanted to list some things out.

1. **Where do you live?**

Do you have access to a decent hospital and hematologist? Your doctor doesn't need to be a thalassemia expert, it would be nice but unless you live in an urban area it's not likely. Having a doctor that is willing to do a little research and learn from those that are experts is awesome. I have told you we have THE. BEST. PHYSICIAN'S ASSISTANT. EVER! He even read the Standards of Care for Thalassemia while on a cruise. If I have an issue in the three weeks between transfusions, he is just an email away.

2. **How willing are you to travel?**

It's a good idea to visit one of the Thalassemia Centers at least once a year. They are:
Children's Healthcare of Atlanta in Atlanta, GA
The Children's Hospital of Boston in Boston, Massachusetts
The Children's Hospital of Los Angeles in Los Angeles, California
The Children's Hospital of Oakland in Oakland, California
The Children's Hospital of Philadelphia in Philadelphia, Pennsylvania
Lurie Children's Memorial Hospital in Chicago, Illinois
Weill Medical College of Cornell University in New York, New York

That being said, you don't need to be near a big city. I have met families at thalassemia conferences that lived in other parts of the country more rural than where I live and they make it work.

3. **How's your insurance?**

My girls require blood transfusions every 3 weeks that includes blood tests. Plus there in lots of yearly testing that needs to be done, not just blood tests but MRIs, eye exams, hearing test etc. After so many transfusions there is an unavoidable iron overload that has to be dealt with, that means a daily chelation medication. Suffice to say it is a very expensive medication. Insurance comes into play here in a big way. Some states have a chronic care insurance (Katie Beckett is a widespread one). A little research would pay off in a big way. Pennsylvania has an awesome program.

4. **How comfortable are you with medical things?**

Maybe this should have been #1, but if you are considering a special needs adoption I'm assuming you have thought about this. Personally, I am pretty comfortable. Hubby is working thru his aversions. My girls get stuck ALOT! Belle has a port; Betty-June does not so there are varying levels of sticks, and it doesn't pay to be squeamish. If you are considering adopting, you are planning to be a parent so you know there will be different things you have to deal with along the lines of body fluids like vomit or urine but how do you feel about blood? Just let that sink in.

At one of Belle's transfusion she fell asleep (as she sometimes does). And when she sleeps, she sweats. This particular time she sweat so much it dislodged the dressing around her port and she de-accessed it in her sleep, all the while the IV machine was pumping, pumping, pumping. When I noticed it her shirt was soaked. I called the nurse and picked Belle up because by now she was starting to cry. We took care of it, the nurse was able to re-access the port, we got Belle changed and it was really no big deal. After the 'crisis' passed the nurse and I noticed I had blood all over my hands. I took a diaper wipe and wiped it off, then washed my hands with soap and water. The nurse commented on how calm I was. I told her, "We are putting that blood IN my kid, on my hands is no big deal."

5. Can you commit time?

My girls go to Children's Hospital for a whole day every 3 weeks, at least. There are also other tests that happen annually such as MRIs, EKGs, Echocardiograms, Ophthalmologist, and Audiologist etc. But it is at least 1 whole day every 3 weeks. We get there between 9 and 10 the girls get accessed and have blood drawn for type and cross as well as other test. The blood gets there about 2 hours later and runs for 3 hours. Some, who live closer to their hospitals, get the blood draw a day or 2 before and the blood is waiting for them when they arrive on transfusion day thus eliminating several hours.

But our transfusion days, at least to me, are not so bad. The girls and I snack, watch movies, play games, color and just have a grand old time. I don't have to worry about laundry, or cleaning or anything else except them. And on the way back to our small town from the big city we stop at the Asian grocery and load up on frozen dumplings, noodles, milk drink and other goodies.

6. Are you ready to deal with the variables?

Kids coming home from other countries (in my experience China) will have had varying degrees and qualities of medical care. Belle was younger (19 months old) and appeared to have pretty good care. Betty-June was older (7 years old) and her care was not as good, plus she has a different form of thalassemia. Older kids coming home are going to be facing more significant iron overload. Also some of these older kids have varying levels of PTSD from their experiences.

7. How do you feel about research?

You will be your child's best advocate. Knowledge is power.

8. Are you prepared to lose your heart?

Because these kids will steal it.

Our family has found this special need manageable. So much so we now have two daughters with thalassemia in our family.

Betty June's sweet face spoke to us. Again we followed our heart and let things fall into place.

If you decide to adopt a child with thalassemia there are lots of resources available. Cooley's Anemia Foundation is a tremendous resource. Eileen is the patient care coordinator and she is really helpful finding a doctor or just getting you good info.

The Facebook group to follow my girls' life with thalassemia is *Blood Sisters Belle and Betty-June*

And if you do decide to jump in with both feet and get Pre-Approval for a child with thalassemia, there is an awesome Facebook group of moms (and dads) ready and willing to help.

Chapter 24

If evolution really works, how come
mothers only have two hands?
- Milton Berle

Tax season came once again like it does every
year. With Betty June settled into a school routine it
became clear that it was once again time for me to return
to working in Matt's office. Since Belle had been home
for almost 18 months I felt it was ok for me to go back full
time this year. Belle split her time between my mother
and Matt's mother.

I was concerned about spending too much time
away from Betty June since she was so newly home and
still learning to trust us. I wanted to be able to pick her up
from school as much as possible. Matt and I talked it over
and came to a rough solution; I would try to get to work
between 6 and 6:30 AM so I could leave by 2. Having
never been accused of being a morning person, this was no
small task for me but thanks to big sister Serenity we all
made it work.

The night before Serenity helped Betty June
choose her clothes for the next day and together, they
packed their lunches. We all went to bed early because I
got up between 4:30 and 5. I tried to leave the house by
5:30, some days I was more successful than others.
Serenity got herself and Betty June up and dressed while
Daddy dressed Belle and made breakfast for them. They
were all out the door by 7:30 to do drop offs. By the time
Matt got to the office between 8:30 and 9 I had been there
almost 3 hours.

I kissed him goodbye by 2 o'clock and was off to do it all in reverse. He got home around 7:30 and we were all back in bed by 9, girls to sleep and parents for a little TV then sleepy time.

I have the utmost respect for moms that work full time year round. Ladies, you rock! Keeping up this pace, even for a few months, seriously knocked me for a loop.

Our whole family was happy to see April 15th roll around so our lives could return to our version of normal. Just like other life events don't happen in a bubble, tax season doesn't either. Life keeps happening January through April. This year saw many events.

After the New Year Betty June was baptized by the same minister that had baptized Belle. Since she was older I spent some time trying to explain what it meant to her. I searched YouTube for videos of baptism for her to watch. On Sunday January 18th wearing our Chinese silks, Betty June was baptized. I'm not sure she understood everything it meant; actually I'm pretty sure she didn't, but we knew. And there were plenty of tears of joy that cold, January morning shed by the church that had been praying for her for so long.

In February big brothers, Donovan and Matthew moved out of our house. The boys got an apartment together in our small town. I had a good cry over that. Mattie was/is my first baby. Donovan is my baby boy. I hugged them and hated to let them go. That evening Matt realized that for the first time since we became parents, he was the only male in our household. With red puffy eyes from crying I enjoyed a wicked laugh.

In March we took the girls to see Disney on Ice. Like most girls around the country in 2015, our girls have been swept away in the phenomenon that is the movie Frozen. The little girls have decided that Betty June is Elsa, Belle is Anna and big sister, Serenity, is Olaf. I'm sorry Serenity, there was a meeting and a vote and those were the results, but cheer up! Olaf gets the best one-liners. Belle and Betty June wore the Elsa and Anna dresses they had received for Christmas, as did most of the little girls in the arena, and keeping in the spirit Serenity wore an Olaf shirt. Half the show was dedicated to "Frozen" and when Elsa came out to skate to 'Let It Go' every little girl in the arena sang along. It was very moving. This was also a very important event because we were working pretty diligently to 'Disneyfy' Betty June in preparation for April's big event, her first trip to Walt Disney World.

March also brought St. Patrick's Day. That morning Betty June wanted to wear her purple Ariel shirt to school (the Disnification was working). I had a hard time convincing her to wear a green shirt. She just didn't understand why. It became that awkward moment when you try to explain to your 7 year old Chinese daughter that on March 17 Americans wear green and everyone pretends to be Irish.

March also brought a rather odd event. I was just finishing up my work day when my cell phone rang. It was 'My Michael' asking if we were in the emergency room. He had received a call telling him Isabelle Dailey was being seen in the ER. We both thought that was really strange because I was at work and Belle was with her grandmother. When I asked him at the next transfusion he told me there was another little girl that was a patient at the hospital named Isabell**A** Dailey but Dailey was spelled different. It turned out to be a really good thing that incident happened. We will see why later.

April brought Easter and all the hoopla that accompanies it. The Saturday before Easter we dye eggs. Why? Because when I was a little girl we dyed eggs the Saturday before Easter because when my mom was a little girl they dyed eggs the Saturday before Easter…

It can be difficult and humorous to explain why we do the things we do. And, in fact, it really makes you think about your traditions. I love a tradition, maybe that is why we have so many in our family. If it's worth doing, it's worth making it a tradition!

Chapter 25

No, I never saw an angel, but it is irrelevant whether I saw one or not. I feel their presence around me.
Paulo Coelho

When we dye eggs for Easter we really dye eggs for Easter. My mom comes over to help and Matt's mom comes over. Unfortunately many years Daddy misses it because it falls during tax season. Such was the case this year.

After we finished dying dozens of eggs the grandmothers both went home to continue Easter preparations. Our ham was in the refrigerator waiting to be cooked for tomorrow's feast. The sisters were playing when I noticed Belle not looking like herself and she was being pretty whiney. When I picked her up I noticed she was pretty warm so I took her temperature. It was 100.5, the start of something. I had just got over an upper respiratory infection so assumed that was Belle's issue, but I kept taking her temperature and it fluctuated but never dropped below 100. In most kids this would not be an issue, a dose of Tylenol or Motrin, and a little rest is all they would need, but Belle has a port so things get more complicated.

I called Children's Hospital and spoke to the hematologist on call and was told to take Belle to the emergency department, they would call ahead. Because Belle is so young and has a small size port our local hospital didn't keep small enough Huber needles to access her port, as a result, Children's had given me one to carry with us for just such an occasion. One blood culture and a Rocephin IV through the port later we were headed home by 3:30.

The rest of the evening went along with no excitement other than the excitement the eve of a big holiday brings. We were spending a lot of time explaining to Betty June what to expect the next day. She had a hard time understanding why a giant rabbit would bring her a basket of candy to celebrate the Resurrection of Jesus but if she was getting candy it was all good.

Belle woke me up at 5:30 AM with a fever of 105. The Rocephin IV she had received the day before has 24 hour coverage so spiking such a high temperature so soon was a big deal. Fortunately Grandma and Poppy live right next door so they were nearby to stay with the other girls.

Another call to Children's and another trip to the emergency room equaled a very scared mommy. Since we had already used the only Huber needle I had they were unable to access her port so they just gave her a shot of antibiotic in her thigh as we were heading out the door of the emergency department to get into a waiting ambulance for a trip to Children's Hospital of Pittsburgh.

Every parent gets scared when their child is sick. If your child has a chronic illness you get a little more scared, but I want to tell you why I was extra scared this Easter Sunday.

I have told you before that there are approximately 1000 transfusion dependant thalassemia patients in the United States. With the advent of social media many of those patients and their families 'know' each other. At last year's CAF Conference I met several parents of tiny thalassemia tots like my Belle. I was able to connect with them on Facebook and follow them and their kid's lives. Their victories were our victories, their setbacks were our setbacks.

In January the unthinkable happened, we lost Baby Z. It started with a cold after Christmas, progressed to RSV and it seemed like in no time at all she was gone forever. She was just a little younger than Belle. I had spoken to her mother only briefly the previous June but my 'sister' had to bury her baby and our little thalassemia community was rocked. I thought about Baby Z a great deal that Resurrection Sunday.

Now here I was on Easter morning in an ambulance heading to Children's Hospital in Pittsburgh with my baby. Viral pneumonia, urinary tract infection, hemoglobin of 9.5 were all the things our local hospital had told me, prepare to stay in Pittsburgh a while. I accompanied Belle who fell asleep in her car seat attached to a gurney while Matt went home to gather things we would need for a hospital stay, put out Easter goodies for the girls and call our pastor.

When we got to the ER at Children's the ambulance team began giving report to the ER team. They started with 'Isabella Dailey age 3'. Remembering the mix up that had happened a few weeks ago I immediately corrected them; this is Isabelle Dailey, not Isabella. I don't like to be 'that' mom that insists on correct pronunciation of a name but in this instance I felt it was very important. I tried to make sure the triage person understood. We were put into a room and everything started happening. Nurses were in and out taking health history and vitals. She went for another chest x-ray because the compact disc of x-ray copies our local hospital had sent them was blank. We were waiting for dad when a whole group of doctors came in with the main doctor giving them her case. "Isabella Dailey age 3 history of tracheotomy, blah, blah" No! I stopped him. This is ISABELLE Dailey, she doesn't have a tracheotomy, and she never had a tracheotomy. She has beta thalassemia major and a port. He looked disappointed and left. So much for making sure triage had the right file.

We had reached out to friends and family via Facebook and church to ask for prayers for Belle and it worked. In Pittsburgh they saw no signs of pneumonia or urinary tract infection. Her hgb was low and she was slightly dehydrated. They had re-accessed her port for a blood culture and were giving her IV fluids. We were able to go home to enjoy the rest of Easter with our family. Belle fell asleep on the way home and slept for most of the rest of the day.

I stayed home from work Monday with her but went back to work Tuesday. Since she was staying with Matt's mom, a retired nurse practitioner, I felt somewhat confident. She understood to call us if Belle got another temperature. And she called us. I once again called Pittsburgh and was told to take her back to the emergency room. Once back at our local ER I did get a rather pleasant surprise, they had started stocking pediatric Huber needles! Belle received yet another round of Rocephin and we headed back home.

By now Belle's hgb had understandably tanked. She was down to 7.5, the lowest she had been since coming home from China. She had been a very sick little girl and the fevers had burned through her hemoglobin. But she was on the mend now and getting better, she kicked whatever virus had been plaguing her and was ready to visit her buddy, Mickey Mouse, at the end of the month!

Chapter 26
All our dreams can come true, if we have the courage to pursue them.
Walt Disney

Yes, we were going to Walt Disney World, again. After tax season we try to take a vacation to celebrate getting through another year. I have told you our family has a special place in our hearts for Walt Disney World and we wanted to share the magic with Betty June. Matt's mom and dad went with us this time and we had rented a vacation home with its own pool. We had big plans for good times.

Did someone mention plans? I love planning our trips. I love researching, reading, digging for good info and choosing our events. This trip was no different.

As part of the Disneyfication of Betty June we watched the entire collection of Princess Movies, Frozen, Snow White, Aladdin, Beauty and the Beast, Tangled, all of them, but the one that captured Betty June's heart and mind was Cinderella. All the girls love Frozen but they also each have their personal princess. Serenity claims Mulan and Belle claims Belle from Beauty and the Beast, but Betty June is all about the princess in blue, Cinderella.

I decided that taking the girls to Bippity Boppity Boutique in Downtown Disney would be a fun experience for us all and provide some great photo opportunities. In preparation for the trip I ordered Betty June a Cinderella dress to go along with Belle's Belle gown. All three girls had their hair done at the Boutique along with their make-up and nails. Belle and Serenity loved it, Betty June didn't seem to understand all the fuss but they were all so beautiful. After their appointments we walked a little way to the photography studio to have professional pictures done of the girls.

If a girl is all dolled up you just have to take her out on the town, right? We drove to the Grand Floridian Hotel to have dinner at 1900 Park Fare with the blue princess herself, Cinderella. Along with Cinderella was Prince Charming, Drusilla and Anastasia, the step-sisters, and Lady Tremaine, the stepmother. Betty June had been pretty excited to actually meet Cinderella. She looked through her coloring books to find a picture of Cinderella dancing with Prince Charming and she carefully colored it to give to Cinderella that evening. It was going to be magical, I thought.

When we were seated at the restaurant Betty June asked me why we were doing all this, the dress, Bippity Boppity Boutique, dinner with Cinderella. I told her we were doing it because I knew she really liked Cinderella and I wanted to make sure she got to meet her. I told her I loved her and wanted to make her happy. She was so nervous/excited she forgot to give Cinderella the picture. So after our meal Daddy took the sisters to the lobby while our waiter brought Cinderella back to our table to receive the lovingly colored picture. Cinderella was so kind and gracious as she thanked Betty June over and over promising to show the Prince.

That night Betty June had another grieving session. She didn't understand why we would want to make her happy. She didn't think she was special or deserved to be happy. It was bad. I think it was really bad. She had heard so much negative talk about herself and she believed it all. I know thalassemia carries a stigma in many countries and people with thalassemia are considered to be a drain on the family. Somewhere along the line Betty June had become convinced of her unworthiness. The beautiful dress, the fancy hair, the special dinner she felt like she didn't deserve any of it. We spent a lot of time that night trying to correct that idea.

Betty June is special.

Betty June deserves to be happy.

Betty June deserves to be loved.

For seven years she was convinced she was unworthy of love and adoration. She WAS Cinderella in her mind. Remember at the tender age of 5 she was left at a hospital by her birth family. I want to believe she was left for all the noblest reasons, but that is me not her. It is her pain and hers alone. It is our job to fill her love cup to overflowing because,

Betty June is special.

Betty June deserves to be happy.

Betty June deserves to be loved.

We had her repeat those phrases after us over and over again. We want to empty her emotional cup of all the muck and yuckiness and refill it with love, hopes, dreams and all things good.

In the end she was as smitten with Disney as the rest of us. She loved the thrill rides, the faster it went the more she liked it, but in an unusual turn of events, it was the carousel she wasn't so sure about. Maybe she felt like she had experienced enough ups and downs.

Chapter 27

Gratitude can transform common days into thanksgivings, turn routine jobs into joy, and change ordinary opportunities into blessings.
William Arthur Ward

So our life is chugging along quite well now. Every three weeks we visit Children's Hospital of Pittsburgh. Twice a year we are seen at Children's Hospital of Philadelphia.

A typical transfusion day starts pretty early. Usually our appointment is at 9 or 9:30 AM, so we need to leave our house by 7 AM to allow for travel time and rush hour. The girls must be out of bed by 6 to make it out the door in time so I am up by 5:30 to get ready first. Everyone gets a quick breakfast, Exjade and I put the numbing cream on Belle's port and cover it with a dressing. We gather up the Kindle, my Chrome book, cords, headphones, coloring books, crayons, and anything else we may need(because I probably forgot to do it the night before) and load us and it into the car. I hope they will fall back to sleep on the trip down and I listen to a podcast on the drive. We inevitably hit some rush hour traffic as we get closer to the city.

I get a ticket as I enter the parking garage and find a spot. One of the best things about getting there relatively early is it isn't too hard to find a parking spot. We still use a stroller for these days just to carry 'stuff'. I load everything onto our beast of burden and go into the hospital.

Betty June is our self appointed 'elevator girl'. She loves to push the buttons and Belle isn't interested in challenging her yet.

We check in at the first desk to get security stickers. Each of us gets a bright yellow name sticker to wear. From there we have to stop at the kiosk to buy 2 bags of white cheddar popcorn for the day, say hello to the security guard and wait for another elevator to take us to the 9th floor.

Off the elevator, through the double doors and another check in desk are next in our routine. The ladies working this desk know us well by now. We have seen one go from a new trainee to trainer and seen another through her pregnancy and maternity leave. There we check in for the girls' transfusions and get little green circle stickers to show we haven't been out of the country in the last three weeks and a buzzer.

Another set of double doors stands between us and the waiting room. The waiting room is a brightly colored room with iPad stations, a book cart with books donated by a local book store for kids to take home and TVs permanently tuned to kiddie TV.

Once the buzzer goes off the girls and I go through still more double doors to triage. There the girls are weighed and measured. They have their blood pressure taken as well as their temperature. Once I had no idea Belle was getting sick until she had a temperature in triage. That was an exciting day because Belle started vomiting not too long after. Thankfully we were in a place with an attentive medical staff and a cleaning staff!

After triage it is down the hall, through more double doors and the girls take off running to the nurse's station for hugs. The girls greet everyone they know while I follow after them pushing the stroller. Everyone is happy to see each other and the girls chatter away.

On the way to the infusion bay we pass the kitchen/snack room. The room has a full size refrigerator, ice machine, small chest freezer, Keurig and stocked cabinets. The fridge is full of drinks, sodas, juice, and milk. The chest freezer is full of popsicles. There are also graham crackers, saltines, peanut butter, condiments etc. We visit this room plenty during our stay.

We go into the infusion bay and choose our spot. The infusion bay is a huge room that is divided by curtains into treatment areas. We choose a spot with a cot and recliner. If daddy is with us we take two areas, one for each girl and parent, but if it is just me with them I find it easier to corral them in a single area.

Some areas have just a recliner and additional chair or two. Some areas have a hospital cot with chairs. All areas have a table, TV and Wii (donated by Mario Lemieux Foundation).

We set up 'camp' in our area. Usually the girls take off their shoes and both get on the bed. We pull the TV on its arm from the wall and find a movie. Each TV has a selection of movies for kids and parents as well as TV stations and games available. We almost always start with Frozen.

Betty June's nurse calls for the IV team to come up and start her IV and do the blood draw. Belle's nurse comes in to access her port. Usually Belle cries on principle, but she sits on my lap, we take off her shirt, or unzip it as the nurse prepares. Once the Huber needle is secured the nurse starts drawing tubes of blood. By now Belle has calmed down and wants to help as each tube is filled Belle shakes it. After all the tubes are drawn Belle helps flush her line by pushing the plunger on the syringe. When the IV team come to access Betty June I stand beside the bed and hold her hand. The IV team has lots of tricks in their bag to find her best vein. She cries a little but is really very brave. She doesn't try to pull her arm away or even flinch. I am always amazed by the way she handles it, she may cry but she never fights it. Once the IV is in, the blood is drawn and she is taped up to wait out the day. The blood will go through a type and cross to double check their blood type and any antibodies they may have developed as well as checking ferritin, kidney function, liver function and other things.

By now we have probably seen 'My Michael' at least once just to say hello and discuss anything that may have been going on since our last visit. If we have time we go down to the cafeteria to get a few more provisions for the day.

We will see 'My Michael' again once the hemoglobin level is back. Once we know that he can officially order the blood. The ferritin takes a little longer to come back.

It takes about two hours for the blood to arrive from the blood bank. At the beginning of the week the clinic sends a patient list to the blood bank that way they are prepared. If they don't send the list it can be a grueling wait for blood. That has happened to us, Betty June was scheduled but somehow Belle wasn't on the list, even though she needed transfused also. Just as Betty June was nearing the end of her transfusion Belle's blood arrived. We closed down the clinic that day.

Once the blood is running we have three hours until it is done. Fortunately the pump is on a mobile IV pole. We pass the time with trips to the snack room, coloring, movies, stickers, play-doh, and bubbles, whatever it takes to keep them happy. The child life team brings them goodies to help keep them occupied also. Some days we are visited by a therapy dog.

During the time the blood is running the girls have vitals done every quarter hour for the first hour then every hour. Hopefully Belle may fall asleep but usually not.

We will probably see 'My Michael' one more time

before the transfusion is finished to discuss our next visit. This usually means we both have our iPhones out looking at calendars and counting days until we agree on a day. Once the blood is finished the IV is pulled, the port is de-accessed and we are almost free. 'My Michael' will print out our discharge papers and the girls will visit the treasure chest for a prize.

We go back down the hall to the check in desk to make the next appointments if it is before 5pm. If it is after 5 I leave the paper on the desk to wait for a call. Usually it is between 4 and 5 and I can make the appointment.

After I get everybody and everything loaded into the car I leave the parking garage using a prepaid ticket I received from the check-in desk. Fortunately there is a fund that pays the parking fee for patients in the infusion clinic; otherwise it would cost $20.

We usually find ourselves leaving Pittsburgh during the evening rush hour but that doesn't stop us from making a stop at the Asian grocery store. Belle will be fighting sleep once in her car seat, it is Betty June's job to keep her awake until we get to the store.

At the market we load up on convenience Asian food for the girls. Usually we get a case of 'Want Want' milk in red cans, frozen dumplings, noodles, spices and some candy. We are becoming well known at 'our' Asian market. Maybe we stand out because of our racial makeup, white parents/Chinese children, but I find that kind of hard to believe in a city like Pittsburgh. Once I stopped there with Betty June after one of her procedures without Belle. At the checkout counter the Asian cashier asked, "Where you baby?" So now I am very conscience when we are in the store and do my best to represent the adoption community in the best light. From trying to use my pitiful Mandarin skills by saying hello, thank you and goodbye in Mandarin to using two hands to pass the cashier my credit card. I say try because we are still human and last time Betty June threw up just before we got to the checkout. Thank goodness that was a time Matt was with us. But after an average shopping trip, I toss our purchases into the trunk with the ever expanding pile of stuff.

But we aren't done quite yet. As part of living with thalassemia I try extra hard to make sure the girls (and as a result, us) eat a healthy diet. I can get most things local but since we are in the big city a stop at Trader Joe's and maybe Whole Foods is in order. I love to get good organic produce and healthy snacks for them. After those stops it is back towards home we go.

Both girls will fall asleep on the way home. When we finally turn onto our road it will be close to 7pm, sometimes later making it a 12 hour day. I will carry Belle in and lay her on the couch and she very well may sleep the rest of the night. Matt and Serenity will carry in our goodies and we will all put away the groceries. Usually Matt will have dinner waiting for us and we happily devour it. Transfusion day means we all hit the sheets early because it has been a long day.

Our days in the infusion clinic can be long and hectic but I am so thankful for them. Because of those long days and the yucky daily medicine, my girls have the hope of a bright future. It wasn't too long ago that parents of children with thalassemia were given a bleak outlook. I met a 62 year old man with beta thalassemia major who said his parents were told he wouldn't make it to 11 years old.

I'll take the long days.

Chapter 28

The truth is you don't know what is
going to happen tomorrow.
Life is a crazy ride, and nothing is
guaranteed.
Eminem

So thalassemia is now a part of our lives.
Sometimes it is a big part and sometimes it isn't. We still
do all the things we used to do but now it may take a little
more planning.

We still travel as much as we can. Right now we
are planning a three week trip to Paris, Disneyland Paris,
Barcelona and a transatlantic cruise home. Why three
weeks? Because that is as long as we can go between
transfusions without issues. Each trip we plan now we
take Belle and Betty June's transfusion schedule into
consideration. I also do a little extra research to make the
trip work for us. One thing I need to know is where the
nearest children's hospital is, (Hospital Necker in Paris).

In America thalassemia is not the death sentence it
can be in other parts of the world. When we brought home
Belle I assumed that she could not have biological
children. That wasn't a big deal to me because as you may
have guessed, I think adoption is a wonderful way to build
a family. I was pretty surprised at our first visit to CHOP
to find out I was wrong about that. Biological children
ARE possible. It may not be easy and there are things you
need to do to prepare your body, but it can and does
happen.

In the interest of full disclosure life with thalassemia is not all sunshine and lollipops. As I write this we are in the midst of deciding if Betty June can keep her spleen. It was really enlarged when we came home from China. After consulting with our thalassemia team and a surgeon it was decided we would wait and see how her spleen would respond to a good transfusion schedule. With the size it was when she came home, the surgeon was not sure he could do the surgery laparoscopically. So if it at least shrunk some her surgery and recovery would be easier. Now at 9 months home it does not appear to have shrunk at all. We are traveling back to Philadelphia in a few weeks for our semi-annual trip after which we will make a plan of action. Fortunately the type of thalassemia Betty June has is one that responds well to removing the spleen. Sometimes if a person with HGB H disease gets the spleen removed they are no longer transfusion dependant. They are able to maintain a hgb around 9 and live a normal life. For Betty June we would probably continue transfusions at least for now to help her growth.

After our first visit to CHOP we received their report in the mail. Of all the things in that medical report to break my heart was one line, one diagnosis I was not expecting, FAILURE TO THRIVE. At 7 years old Betty June was 42 inches tall and 38 pounds. I know it's silly to let something like that bother me. There were so many factors that went into why she was as small as she is genetics, lack of proper transfusions, being in an orphanage, poor nutrition… But in order to help her grow and thrive we would want to keep her hemoglobin higher than she could maintain on her own.

And Belle, well, at the last transfusion she had blood in her urine. And continuing the theme of 'no easy answers' we aren't sure why. She had bladder surgery in China and because of that we do a yearly visit to an urologist. We had been told by the urologist that because of the surgery we could expect a few things:

1. She would be a slow potty trainer. At 3 years 5 months she is in 'big girl undies' during the day with very few incidents. We still don't completely trust her at night but have forgotten to put her in a pull up a few nights and we all woke up dry.

2. She would be prone to urinary tract infections. She has had more than her share of those but we are hopeful now that she is out of diapers that will help.

3. She has potential for kidney stones.

Oh yes, and did I mention that one of the potential side effects of Exjade, her daily chelation medication, is kidney stones? And urinary tract infections can cause blood in the urine.

So now we are following up with a nephrotologist, kidney specialist, to see if we can figure this out.

Some days it is harder to get Betty June's IV in than others. Some days Belle resists having her port accessed and struggles against it. There are complications with medications or scheduling conflicts. Fevers send us to the hospital and we find ourselves second guessing ourselves all the time. "Is Belle being grumpy and naughty because she doesn't feel good or because she is 3 years old?" "Should I hold and cuddle her to make her feel better or give her a timeout?" If you haven't figured out by now, I would choose cuddle every time.

And what would a discussion about healthcare be without talking about insurance. I am very fortunate to have a husband that while squeamish in the medical arena is cunning as a fox in the business world. He deals with all the insurance issues. That is no small task!

Children's Hospital of Philadelphia Thalassemia Clinic has a social worker that deals with insurance companies on behalf of their patients. That is his job, that is all he does. I hope he gets paid really well.

When we first went to Philadelphia with Belle we had pre-approval, the hospital had a copy of the pre-approval, and the social worker had a copy of the pre-approval. We went to Philadelphia and Belle had her appointments and blood tests with no issue. That is until the insurance company figured out we lived in the western part of the state and Philadelphia is in the eastern part of the state. So despite having pre-approval the claims were all denied. That little struggle is still being fought between CHOP and the insurance company.

As big a pain as insurance companies can be, they are super important. If we were paying cash for the girls' Exjade it would cost just under $10,000, and that is just one facet of their care!

So Matt fills out all those icky insurance forms and I write N/A on lots of health histories, schedule appointments and take the girls to the appointments. Teamwork.

No, dealing with a chronic illness isn't always easy. Not long after we were home with Belle she and I were at one of her transfusions. The nurse practioner sat down across from me and said, "Now tell me, how are YOU are doing?" I will admit I was slightly taken aback at this question. I told her, "I chose this.", and that was the truth. I chose to deal with blood transfusions and chelation the same way I chose to deal with diapers and bottles. That is not to say that many times I feel like I am in way over my head, but I never regret my decision to jump in the pool.

Chapter 29

The process of spotting fear and refusing to obey it is the source of all true empowerment.
Martha Beck

Empowerment is a word we hear tossed about quite a bit these days. It seems like everyone wants empowerment. We all want to empower others. But how do we do that? Especially in the case of chronically ill children, the question looms large.

My girls are pretty young, 7 and 3. Being such young children, there is not much in their lives they have power or authority over especially with respect to health care. They MUST be transfused regularly. They MUST take their chelation medication every day. For those two items there is no choice.

Right now it is mom and dad that control those big things. I make the appointments. I drive them to the hospital. I prepare the Exjade every morning and make sure they drink it.

I'm no expert, just a mom trying to do what is best for her family. As such I have done some research and came up with "Mom's 5 Steps to Empowered Children".

1.   Give them "Either/Or" choices.
2.   Give them opportunities to succeed
3.   Give them knowledge
4.   Give them a voice
5.   Give them people

Give them Either/Or choices

To ease them into some autonomy, we try to give them choices where we can. "Do you want juice or tea for your Exjade?" "Which arm would you like them to check first for your IV, Betty-June?" "Belle, should we say 1, 2, 3 or A, B, C for the port access?" These are either/or questions. There is no negotiating that the IV and port access will happen but there is a choice how it will happen.

Give them opportunities to succeed

I have read that sometimes adults with chronic illness feel like failures due to their illness. I know I felt like that after my third miscarriage. I felt like my body was betraying me.

I don't ever want Belle or Betty June to feel like that so I look for things or ways they can feel like winners. Performing a song they have learned for grandma and grandpa makes my girls feel like superstars. Several years ago we moved the dishes from a high cupboard in the kitchen to a low cupboard so the kids could unload the dishwasher. Betty June is very proud of the fact she can unload the dishwasher 'all by herself'. Everyday Belle gives our doggie his dry dog food 'all by herself'. These are two small instances that the girls really feel in control. Plus they are learning that they can help others.

Give them knowledge

When Betty June was learning English, she referred to IVs as 'Ow Ow Ows'. It was cute and we used it for a while until she learned enough English to use the correct names. Knowledge is power and knowing the correct names for things gives the girls' power. We use their words to explain things. Belle calls her port her 'Magic Button'. I may tell her that her 'Magic Button' is a port. They hear words like 'thalassemia', 'blood', 'transfusion' and 'chelation' all the time. There is no frightening power to these words, no secrecy and certainly no stigma.

Give them voice

It is important to hear what they say. IVs DO hurt. Sometimes hospitals ARE scary. What these kids are feeling is very real to them. Minimizing what they think or feel cannot possibly help them.

Not only do we need to hear what they say but they should be able to ask questions of their care providers. At the last Cooley's Anemia conference we attended the doctors held a question and answer session with the children. The kids could ask these doctors anything. One little girl asked if children with thalassemia needed to brush their teeth. Who knows where that particular question was born? (I would love to hear the back story) But she wanted to know and deserved an answer. So the world class hematologist, with a straight face, answered her. He heard her, affirmed her and answered her. She deserved no less.

Give them people

According to Barbara Streisand, people who need people are the luckiest people in the world. With all due respect to Ms Streisand, I must correct her; people who *have* people are the luckiest people in the world.

Community is a tremendous gift. Belle and Betty June were the only people they knew that had thalassemia. They had each other, which in and of itself is pretty special, but they were alone. Thanks to attending the

Cooley's Anemia conferences they met other little girls and boys with thalassemia. They met teens, adults and even seniors living, no, THRIVING with thalassemia. They don't need to feel alone.

With the advent of social media and the internet, people with rare conditions can connect daily even though they live hundreds, even thousands, of miles apart. Now my 7 and 3 year olds aren't on Facebook or Instagram but for teens, adults and parents this is such a great support network.

It's not just about other kids with thalassemia but the medical personnel the girls see. Why do they adore 'My Michael' and the nurses? It's because 'My Michael' and the nurses see Belle. 'My Michael' and the nurses see Betty June. They don't see just another patient. They call the girls by their name and talk to them. Betty June adores Nurse Eileen because Nurse Eileen adores her. 'My Michael' and the nurses are their people.

Chapter 30

"A child born to another woman calls me Mom. The depth of the tragedy and magnitude of the privilege are not lost on me" -Jody Landers

I wanted to add just a few words about adopting an older child. Please bear in mind that I have a study group of one. So I do not claim to be an expert, I am just a soldier in the trenches.

We all have scars. I was a pretty active child and have scars on my knees from numerous gravel road wipeouts on my bike. I have a surgery scar from having my tubal reversed. I have a small scar on the right side of my face from having a cyst removed. They are all visible, harmless scars.

My sister has more of an issue with scars. Her scars build up thick tissue. The scars from her cesarean deliveries and her tubal wove a web throughout her abdomen. She had to have additional surgery to remove some of the scar tissue. Her scars were less benign than mine but they were still visible and treatable.

My oldest son, Mattie, has a big scar on his left forearm from surgery on a broken arm as a result of a bicycle accident. It has become a family game to come up with the best made up story to go with that scar. His scar is visible and actually kind of fun.

Physical scars come in all shapes and sizes. Some are harmless, some are fun and some need treatment.

Emotional scars are a different story.

When older children come into our lives through adoption, they bring with them a whole lifetime of memories. Some of those memories are happy, some are indifferent and some are sad, even tragic.

In the case of children with thalassemia, often times they are older when they go to the orphanage. Being abandoned later in their childhood leaves a big ugly scar. When Betty June was crying after a very special day it was because she didn't think she deserved to be so happy. I think that was directly related to the fact she felt like she was left because she was a burden on her birth family. Not only was she a girl, but a sick girl and therefore she thought she was unworthy of good things.

In the case of Chinese adoption, adopting an older child usually goes hand in hand with a medical special need. It is important to be aware of what the long term consequence of lack of proper medical care can be.

Speaking from my experience of adopting a child with thalassemia, it can be significant but reversible. We are still dealing with the issues of Betty June's spleen. But there is also the potential issue of significant iron overload, especially in beta thalassemia major. The lack of proper transfusions led to the enlarged spleen, but it also kept her from being extremely iron overloaded. She still has some iron overload that needs daily chelation but it is not as extreme as some I have seen. Some come home so extremely overloaded they need double chelation, not just Exjade dissolved and drank every day but also daily Deferral via a slow subcutaneous infusion. Also with long term inadequate transfusions there are potential growth issues, for instance Betty June's failure to thrive diagnosis.

Children coming home that have spent years in an orphanage also have the potential to exhibit institutional behavior, some good and some bad. Betty June has a tendency to be very independent and yet very young for her age. This is classic behavior for a child coming from an institution. She will go from wanting total autonomy in choosing clothes or brushing her teeth to wanting to sit on my lap and be rocked. Now some of that comes from being jealous of Belle being on my lap, so it is kind of a tossup sometimes as to what is normal sibling rivalry versus adoption related. Thus is the eternal struggle.

Unfortunately, another side effect of living in an orphanage is kind of a 'survival of the fittest' mentality. It can potentially be pretty scary. I did read about that issue when we were working on Betty June's adoption. That behavior will sometimes manifest itself through food hording, lying, bullying etc. Mercifully, we have been spared any of those behaviors, but we do see some real jealousy. If I am holding Belle, Betty June may pout until Belle moves on and she can climb up on my lap. Or best case scenario, they each get a knee to sit on and I am smothered in cuddles.

Something we have seen is the fear/avoidance of men. Apparently, most of the orphanage staff is female. As a result all my girls took quite some time to warm up to their dad and brothers. In Betty June's case I don't think her birth father was the kindest person so she had a bad feeling towards men in general. With love and perseverance her dad and brothers have won her over.

Ok, now that I have thrown all the 'big bads' at you, let me tell you the amazing positives. Have you ever sat and watched a flower bloom? That is the perfect analogy.

Language is a whole crazy ball of wax. I try to speak a little Mandarin. When I met Betty June in China I tried to talk to her in Mandarin. She laughed at my pitiful attempt. Our communication became a combination of iTranslate, my Mandarin attempts and a wacked out game of charades! But communicate we did, thankfully young brains learn language pretty fast.

Betty June knows her story. For Serenity and Belle, they were babies and only know what we have told them about their babyhood and early childhood. Betty June remembers her birth family and remembers being left at the hospital. She remembers her life at the orphanage. She will remember the day we met and our time together in China.

Just because Belle was younger does not mean she has been spared her share of emotional scars. Belle has some food issues. She needs to know there will be food available. We have stopped putting the snacks away in a cupboard and now leave the boxes sitting on the countertop where she can see them. Sometimes she wants a snack right before dinner. Those times I may give her a snack bar to put in her pocket or just hold. I tell her if she is still hungry after supper she can eat that bar. Just having that snack in her hand can make the difference.

Betty June has blossomed from that first day we met at the Guangdong Civil Affairs office. No longer is she my stoic princess. Now she is a giggly, smiley, girly girl. She loves clothes and shoes, and she thinks the more sparkly the better.

She continues to struggle with self-worth and jealousy. I see how important it is to tell her often how much she is loved, how precious she is, that she deserves to be happy and treated well. I try to give her choices when I can. I look for opportunities for her to succeed and praise her. I know I have critics that say I spoil my kids. But my philosophy has always been: the way to spoil fruit is to put it on a shelf and leave it alone. If the fruit was used for what it was made for (usually a pie in my case) then it never has a chance to spoil. I'm not leaving my kids on a shelf to spoil.

To sum up, older child adoption can be hard, but I firmly believe it is so very worthwhile. In the case of a child with thalassemia, you are quite literally saving their life.

Chapter 31

For there is no friend like a sister in calm or stormy weather; To cheer one on the tedious way, to fetch one if one goes astray, to lift one if one totters down, to strengthen whilst one stands. Christina Rossetti

I am the extremely fortunate mother of 6 children. I am the mother-in-law to one daughter-in-love and quite recently grandmother to a particularly handsome little boy. I have three sons and three daughters, and they are brothers and sisters to their core.Not long after we brought Serenity home from China one of my sons was asked by a buddy if that was his real sister.

His reply was, "She comes in my room and messes with my stuff, she annoys me, she gets me in trouble and I will pound anyone that ever hurts her. Ya, I'd say that makes her my real sister."

The asker was a young teen in this case but curiosity knows no age limits. Because Belle and Betty June have the same special need I am often asked if they are 'real' sisters. Most times it is asked right in front of them.

Example:

"Are they real sisters?"

Me: "They are now."

"But you know, are they really real sisters?"

Now at this point I have a choice to make. Do I hear what the questioner is saying or do I hear what she means? Because of my Southern upbringing I default to the polite answer, most days, and because my girls are within earshot I want to validate their relationship.

Me: "Biologically no they are not but in every other sense they are really real sisters."

This usually satisfies the curious party and we make a quick getaway before there are follow up questions.

I am fortunate enough to have a sister of my own. Ramie is five years younger than me and was born right before Christmas. I thought she was my Christmas present. I loved helping take care of her and giving her bottles. When she was old enough for solid food I felt very grown up feeding her with a spoon. Of course, like older siblings do, I did get annoyed with her and even asked my mother to trade her for a goat. Now, as adults, my sister is my best friend and ally. The fact that we have the same mother and father is really just biology, what makes us really real sisters is so much more.

Belle and Betty June are more than just sisters. They are a built in support system for each other. As they get older and go farther down the road with thalassemia, there will be someone that understands them in a way most could not. Even now when Belle had to be transfused without her really real sister she missed her terribly.

When they play together they will often line up baby dolls and stuffed animals and give them physicals. Some of the doll and animal patients have ports apparently and others need IVs. Toy stethoscopes draped around their necks they explain to the toy patients what is happening. Each girl will be assisting the other in her rounds. Then one sister accesses a port when it should have been an IV, or does a physical on the other sister's doll and a squabble will break out.

Just like really real sisters.

Conclusion

Often when you think you're at the end of something, you're at the beginning of something else.
— Fred Rogers

So, there you have it, our story. Or should I say our story thus far? Our story has really only begun. There is so much life ahead.

Gene therapy is proving to be a real hope for a cure to thalassemia.

There are new chelation drugs on the horizon, even a pill to swallow.

Life expectancies are increasing.

Betty June really wants to learn to ride a bike.

Belle is finally potty trained.

We have a new grandson.

The list goes on and on with no end in sight. Buckle up kiddos, it's gonna be quite a ride!

After almost 50 trips around the sun I can honestly say I am looking forward to everything the good Lord has planned for us. When I was writing that essay in Mr. Cleveland's 11th grade English class, I thought I had a plan for my future. On our wedding day Matt and I thought we had a plan for our future. We wanted 6 kids. That sounded simple enough but we had no idea that plan would involve a single pregnancy, a twin pregnancy, a few miscarriages, and 3 trips to China to build our future. And

while no one dreams of a future that includes a chronically ill child, let alone two, it is a perfect life for us.
I am so glad I wasn't given the future I thought I wanted and instead I was given this life.

Is it perfect?

Would you believe me if I said it was?

Or that is it exactly perfect for us?

The road has been rocky at times. The way wasn't always clear. Mistakes were made and decisions were regretted. We aren't perfect people.

When the Mattie, Dean and Donovan were little my mantra was, "The days are long but the years are short." I had no idea how right I was.

I have six kids, three sons and three daughters.

Three were born in Pennsylvania and three were born in China.

The youngest two have thalassemia.

I wouldn't have it any other way.

Appendix 1

This is a blog post I wrote in December 2004, after we got home from China adopting Serenity.

Isaiah 43:5-7 *Fear not, for I am with you; I will bring your descendants from the East and gather you from the West; I will say to the north 'Give them up!' And to the south 'Do not keep them back!' Bring my sons from afar, and my daughters from the ends of the Earth- Everyone whom I have called by my Name, whom I have created for my Glory; I have formed him, yes, I have made him.*

I have 4 Children. Matthew is the oldest. He was born November 1989 in Butler Pa. I remember many things about that day, Bob Dylan was on the radio on the way to the hospital, and Geraldo Rivera was on the TV in the admission waiting room. I remember this because I don't like either of them very much. It was very late at night when we got to the hospital and he was born the next morning and greeted by lots of family and friends

Dean and Donovan came next. They are twins, identical boys. They were born in October 1991, also in Butler Pa. I remember it was unseasonably warm. We went to the hospital early in the morning and they were born just before noon. Again lots of family and friends were there to welcome them.

Serenity is my daughter. She is also the youngest by 12 years. She was born July 2003 somewhere in the Guangxi Zhuang Autonomous Region, China. But she was born in our hearts long before that. I am not sure who was there when she was born or how she was received but I do know one person that was there....God. He was with her from the beginning saying, my child I made you and I love you. I have a plan for you, it may not be easy but it is right.

A few months later in Sept 03 we were sending all our paperwork, called a dossier, off to China asking the Chinese government for one of their precious children. It arrived in Beijing, China's capital city, at the CCAA, the government division for adoption, and was promptly placed in a stack with all the other foreigners asking to adopt a Chinese child. I can't put my finger on when the desire began to grow within me to adopt a daughter from China but I know it was put there by God. My husband agreed to adopt in Summer 2002 and we began our 'paperchase' in Sept 02. Long before Serenity began to grow in her birth mother's womb, God already had a plan for our lives.

The month after we sent our dossier to China, a family was faced with a very tough decision.
The Chinese government allows only one child per family, in special cases if the first child is a girl they may be allowed to have two. China has the largest population in the world. I read one statistic that says 1 in 4 people on the planet is Chinese. The government felt they had to curb the growth of the population so the made the rule "One child maybe two".

China also has a very strong cultural preference for sons. There is no social security system in place to care for people as they age. Social security is a son to care for you. Sons stay with the family, carry on the name, work the family farm or business. Daughters become part of the husband's family, carrying for them. In poor families this is a big deal.

Back to October 2003, a family, a mother and father, struggle with this policy. Fines are tough for a family breaking the one child law, up to one year worth of income, loss of med privileges, jobs can be lost. Not just parents are punished but extended family as well. So here they have a beautiful, perfect baby girl, maybe she is a second daughter, maybe a first born to very a very poor family. I don't know, but her Maker does and His plan is still in place.

These birth parents must have loved her very much because they took a big risk to leave her in place she would be found. Again punishment is harsh for abandoning a baby. A huge fine, prison time, even forced sterilization if parents are caught. So they had to have tremendous love in their hearts to leave her in so public a place.

Unfortunately their story is not uncommon; it is faced by thousands of parents a year. It would be easy for us Westerners to judge them harshly for what they did, but until we walk a mile in their shoes....

But even as Serenity was left alone, waiting to be found she wasn't really alone. The Maker of Heaven and Earth was there with her, His plan still in place. She was eventually found and taken to an orphanage to wait there for His plan to unfold.

She wasn't the only one waiting. Here in the good ole USA, we were waiting and waiting for what seemed like a very long time. It was 8 months actually, 7 months since Serenity arrived at Yongning SWI, until we received the call telling us we had a daughter, Ning Fu Zhu. Ning is her last name, shared by all the children at Yongning and Fu means Good Fortune. We later would find out that the meaning of her full name is Peaceful Blessing. Well of course we wanted to jump on the first plane we could, but like the rest of the story we had to WAIT.

On July 1st, 2004 at 6:30pm we boarded a plane in PGH and on July 3rd at 6:30 am we landed in Hong Kong. All in all it took 24 hours to get to China and there is a 12 hour time difference. We were greeted by 'Uncle Matthew' a Hong Kong national that would serve as our guide for the next day and a half. We boarded a bus and headed to the Shangri La hotel. It was beautiful beyond belief. Opulent is the word that comes to mind when I remember it.

We signed up for a whirlwind tour of Hong Kong that afternoon. We started with a yummy Dim Sum lunch, then off to see the sights. We saw Victoria's Peak, Aberdeen Fishing Village, I rode a sampan and we toured a pearl jewelry factory before we returned to our hotel at around 6 pm.

Uncle Matthew told us not to fall asleep yet, try to get on China time, stay up until around 10 then go to bed. So what did we do? We fell asleep by 7. But we slept all night and were revived and refreshed by morning.

I left out some important people on this journey. We met up with our travel group in San Francisco, 5 other families to go through this with us. One family like us already had 3 older sons, 1 family had one 6 year old biological son, 1 family was on their second adoption trip to China and 2 were becoming parents for the first time. When we met on July1 we were strangers going to a strange land, but by the time we said good bye we were aunts, uncles, nieces and nephews all with a profound love of Our China

So July 4th we board a plane for Nanning, the city where we would receive Serenity. When we landed in Nanning I was struck by what a land of contrast China is. On one side of the landing strip water buffalo were grazing peacefully, completely uncaring that there were these foreigners coming to bring home daughters, while on the other side of the runway there were 5 Russian built MIGs .

Following us into Nanning was a huge thunderstorm; this would later become a recurring theme to our time in China.

We were met by Michael in Nanning; he would be our guide for the next 6 days, 24 hours a day. He lived with us in the hotel. The Chinese choose their own western names, how fitting he would choose the name of an angel, because he became our guardian angel while we were there. I can't say enough positive things about him. We were taken to our hotel and told to rest because tomorrow was our big day. Gotcha Day

The next day at 3pm we left our hotel, the Majestic, to travel by bus to the Lottery Hotel to receive our babies. That name-Lottery Hotel- has always struck me as a funny name for a place to receive our babies, as if it was all by chance, but it wasn't by chance. This is just another example of God working out his plan for all our lives. Do you think they would change the name to 'God's Plan Hotel'? Neither do I.

Upstairs at the Lottery Hotel 6 babies were waiting for us. To say we were nervous was an understatement, of the 6 families, 2 were waiting to become parents for the first time. I still get goose bumps thinking about that moment. So after a speech by a local official the time has come, in walked 6 nannies carrying 6 beautiful daughters of China. We were the 5th family called. Serenity was handed to me with a worried look on her face, a look she kept for quite a while. Then it was back to the bus and back to the Majestic Hotel to get to know each other.

Now I would like to tell you everything was beautiful. I would like to tell you Serenity was happy to be with her family. I would like to tell you she cooed and smiled from then on. I would like to tell you that but I would be lying. The first 3 days were, shall we say, stressful. Suddenly she found herself with people that looked funny, talked funny, and even smelled funny, and she did not like it one bit. She cried because she didn't want me to hold her, she cried because she didn't want put down. So she and I did the up down dance those first few hours. Dad and Dean made a tactical move that would later be called "The Coca-Cola Maneuver" that is they decided to go for a walk and find a store that sold Coca-Cola. I'm not going to say those first few days were easy, but can I say they were worthwhile. By the fourth day she had decided I was a pretty good nanny and she would keep me.

But the third day was really hard on her, she was sick with bronchitis and grieving mightily, so we missed the side trip to a Buddhist Temple the fourth day because I was afraid of being out in the oppressive heat with a sick and upset baby. In one of the families in our group that went to the temple the dad is a Baptist minister from Mississippi, he told me this story. He did the tour for curiosity sake but when time came for the monks to perform a Buddhist blessing on the girls they hung back. He said, "Homestudy $600, Trip to China $2000, singing 'Jesus Loves Me' to your newly adopted Chinese daughter in a Buddhist temple, priceless!"

I think I should mention the food in Nanning. We ate some meals in the hotel ethnic restaurants, and they were very good. But we ate many dinners from a local restaurant. You may have heard of it, McDonalds. Oh yes, it was very exotic and they delivered.

When we left Nanning we had gone from 6 families of strangers to one large extended family. Holding our babies we bid a tearful goodbye to Michael, our guardian and friend for only 6 days, but he was/is so important to us that we still keep in touch.(edit to add: unfortunately in the time since writing this in 2004, Michael has sadly passed away)

On to Guangzhou we went for the American part of the paperwork. Our guide there was a sprite of a girl called Maggie. We didn't get as close to her as we did our Michael, but she guided us thru our paperwork with awe-inspiring efficiency.

Guangzhou used to be called Canton. It was the only port that foreign trade was allowed. The area we stayed in, Shamain Island was where the English, Dutch and French had their embassies. Now, it is the only city in China that processes American adoption. The western influence can be seen in the buildings and the layout of the island.

We stayed at the White Swan hotel, called the White Stork because of all the American adoptive families that stay there since it is within walking distance to our consulate. Guangzhou was a quick stop because in 3 days we completed all the American requirements of physicals and visa applications, as well as shopping for treasures to share with Serenity when she gets older.

Like the other cities we visited the rains followed us. One time it showed us just how forceful nature can be. We decided on our last full day in China to visit the Guangzhou Zoo. I really wanted to see the pandas. I mean, hey, I came all the way to China and I was missing the Great Wall, I at least wanted to see the pandas! So off we went 3 moms, 2 dads, 4 Chinese little girls and 2 big brothers in 3 taxis to visit some very famous Chinese celebrities, 2 great pandas. Now the taxi ride in and of itself was an experience. I finally just shut my eyes and recited the 23rd Psalm to myself. We arrived at the zoo and paid our admission. Of course the pandas are in the back of the zoo. We found our way to the panda area thanks to the pictures on the signs and there they were 2 of the rarest animals on the planet. But something was wrong.

After looking around I realized WE were the attractions because all the locals were looking at these 3 Caucasian families with these Chinese kids. And then the rains came. At first we thought we could ride it out under a tree, after all I had brought 2 umbrellas in my bag. And then the rains came harder, and harder and HARDER. This time the rain brought along some strong wind and some serious thunder and lightning. All of the sudden metal handled umbrellas did not seem like such a good idea. So we dashed for an overhang of a building to wait it out. I don't know how long we were there but it seemed like an eternity. Wind blew some mulch stuff around and off the top of the building we were standing beside. There was mud and decomposing leaves everywhere.

Once it let up our funny, soggy, little party headed back to the front of the zoo to go back to the White Swan. Along the way we saw metal picnic tables in the lake and several big palm trees uprooted. I actually saw a drown rat just outside the zoo exit, somehow that struck me as poetic. It was definitely time to go home!

After our three days in Guangzhou, whoosh we were back on a plane to Hong Kong, then to San Francisco where Serenity became a US citizen as soon as we touched the ground.

So, Serenity, my youngest child, my daughter, was born in China. I don't know why God chose to have my daughter born in China instead of in Butler, Pa like her brothers, but who am I to question the Almighty? God put China in our lives for a reason. Now we have 2 more holidays on our calendar, Chinese New Year and Autumn Moon Festival. And I hope more global thinking in our minds.

I know Serenity was meant to be our child, just as if she had been born to us, God's plan is infallible. And it is marvelous to see it worked out.

Above– Serenity's
referral picture
from China.

Top Right– Belle
in China

Right– First
picture we ever
saw of Betty June

Above-Girls and I at Disney on Ice

Right-Dad with Belle and Betty June at Magic Kingdom

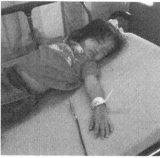

Transfusion
Days

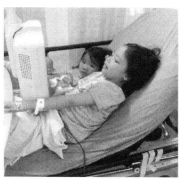

Left– Betty June's Baptism with all the kids and Matt's Mom and Dad

Below– Mother's Day 2015 with all the kids

Bottom Left– Both Grandmothers with Belle and Betty June. Thanksgiving 2014

Belle's Adoption July 2013

Betty June's Adoption
September 2014

First Meeting

Shamain Island Statues

Wearing Red White
And Blue in front of
The American
Consulate

Home with
Daddy and sisters

Braver Than Most

With Poppy (Matt's Dad)
At Betty June's Baptism

With Brother Dean and their new nephew June 2015

Once a Princess, Always a Princess
Walt Disney World April 2015

Mattie,
Donovan and
Dean 2013
July celebration
before we went
for Belle

Mattie and
Serenity
June 2012

Serenity's
special
dance with
Dean at his
wedding.
July 2011.
'You'll Be
in My Heart'

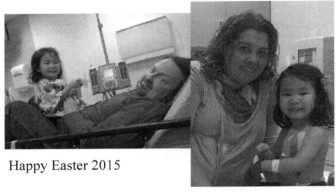

Happy Easter 2015

December 2014 Dental
Surgery

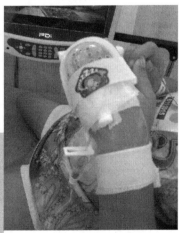

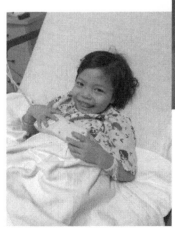

Typical
Betty June
IV

The girls with Mattie

Crazy hair
girls

Mom and girls
camping.
Thalassemia doesn't
slow us down.

About the Author

'Adventure Keeps Calling My Name' is the life motto of Jamie M Dailey. She has traveled to China on 4 adoption trips, three her own and one with a friend. She has cruised through the Panama Canal and stepped foot on 4 continents. But her greatest adventure is raising 6 kids with her husband and best friend, Matthew.

56843287R00104

Made in the USA
San Bernardino, CA
14 November 2017